Beginning
Business Law

Whether you're new to higher education, coming to legal study for the first time or just wondering what Business Law is all about, **Beginning Business Law** is the ideal introduction to help you hit the ground running. Starting with the basics and an overview of each topic, it will help you come to terms with the structure, themes and issues of the subject so that you can begin your Business Law module with confidence.

Adopting a clear and simple approach with legal vocabulary explained in a detailed glossary, Chris Monaghan breaks the subject of Business Law down using practical, everyday examples to make it understandable for anyone, whatever their background. Diagrams and flowcharts simplify complex issues, important cases are identified and explained and on-the- spot questions help you recognise potential issues or debates within the law so that you can contribute in classes with confidence.

Beginning Business Law is an ideal first introduction to the subject for LLB, GDL or ILEX students and especially international students, those enrolled on distance-learning courses or on other degree programmes.

Chris Monaghan is Senior Lecturer in Law at Greenwich University.

D1081318

410110162

Beginning the Law

A new introductory series designed to help you master the basics and progress with confidence.

Beginning Constitutional Law, Nick Howard
Beginning Contract Law, Nicola Monaghan and Chris Monaghan
Beginning Criminal Law, Claudia Carr and Maureen Johnson
Beginning Equity and Trusts, Mohamed Ramjohn
Beginning Employment Law, James Marson
Beginning Evidence, Chanjit Singh Landa
Beginning Human Rights, Howard Davis
Beginning Family Law, Jonathan Herring
Beginning Business Law, Chris Monaghan
Beginning Land Law, Sarah King

Following in Spring 2015
Beginning Medical Law, Claudia Carr

www.routledge.com/cw/beginningthelaw

Beginning
Business Law

CHRIS MONAGHAN

 Routledge
Taylor & Francis Group

LONDON AND NEW YORK

First published 2015
by Routledge
2 Park Square, Milton Park, Abingdon, Oxon OX14 4RN

and by Routledge
711 Third Avenue, New York, NY 10017

Routledge is an imprint of the Taylor & Francis Group, an informa business

British Library Cataloguing in Publication Data
A catalogue record for this book is available from the British Library

Library of Congress Cataloging in Publication Data has been requested.

ISBN: 978-1-138-77986-0 (hbk)
ISBN: 978-1-138-77987-7 (pbk)
ISBN: 978-1-315-77099-4 (ebk)

Typeset in Vectora
by Florence Production Ltd, Stoodleigh, Devon, UK

MIX
Paper from
responsible sources
FSC® C013056
www.fsc.org

Printed and bound in Great Britain by
TJ International Ltd, Padstow, Cornwall

Contents

Table of Cases

Table of Legislation

STATUTORY INSTRUMENTS

Preface

Business law is an exciting area of academic study: you will encounter a variety of interesting areas of the law, such as employment law where you will learn how the courts determine whether someone is an employee and thus has enhanced rights when compared to workers, and how an employer can go about dismissing employees without facing a claim for wrongful dismissal or unfair dismissal. Equally interesting is the law of agency, where you will learn about how it is possible for an agent to enter into a contract and bind their principal (the person on whose account they are entering into contracts with third parties), even where the principal has expressly told the agent that he has no authority to conclude contracts of this type. We shall see that the law of agency applies to all types of businesses, including football clubs and even the film industry.

The key legal principles covered in this book are essential for those who wish to run a business and to avoid the commons pitfalls such as mishandling a redundancy situation, or permitting an agent to abuse her position by failing to keep an eye on what is going on. Equally, those who are advising a business on legal matters must have a thorough understanding of the law and how it relates to the needs of businesses. The aim of *Beginning Business Law* is to provide you with an introduction to the key areas of law that will help you in running or working for a business, or for those intending to have a career in legal practice, where you are advising a business. *Beginning Business Law* is written for students who are studying on non-law degrees and law students who are studying business law and therefore it does not assume prior knowledge. At the end of each chapter you will be directed to useful further reading to help you develop your understanding of the key legal principles explored in the book.

I have been very fortunate to teach students who are genuinely interested in how the law relates to business transactions and the legal implications of business decisions. It is hoped that *Beginning Business Law* will help to make the law accessible to those students who are studying business law for the first time.

I am grateful to my editors Fiona Briden and Damian Mitchell at Routledge for their encouragement and support throughout the writing process. I would also like to thank my project manager Amy Wheeler and copy-editor Jane Fieldsend for their assistance during the production process. Finally, I would also like to thank my anonymous reviewers for their helpful feedback on the text.

This book is dedicated to Sheila.

Any errors are entirely my own. The law is stated as it stood on 1 August 2014.

Chris Monaghan
Senior Lecturer in Law, University of Greenwich

Guide to the Companion Website

www.routledge.com/cw/beginningthelaw

Visit the *Beginning the Law* website to discover a comprehensive range of resources designed to enhance your learning experience.

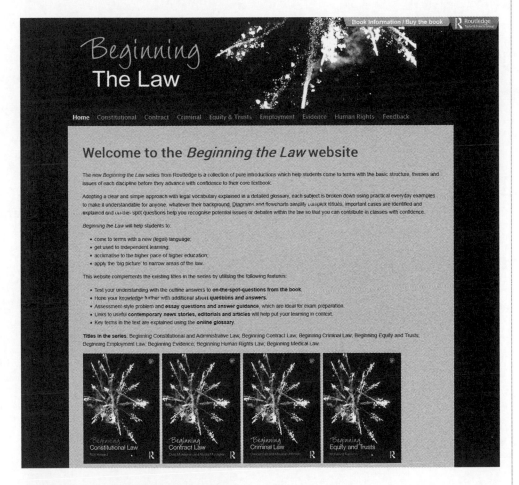

Answers to on-the-spot questions
The author's suggested answers to the questions posed in the book.

Online glossary
Reinforce your legal vocabulary with our online glossary. You can find easy to remember definitions of all key terms, listed by chapter for each title in the *Beginning the Law* series.

Chapter 1
Introduction to business law

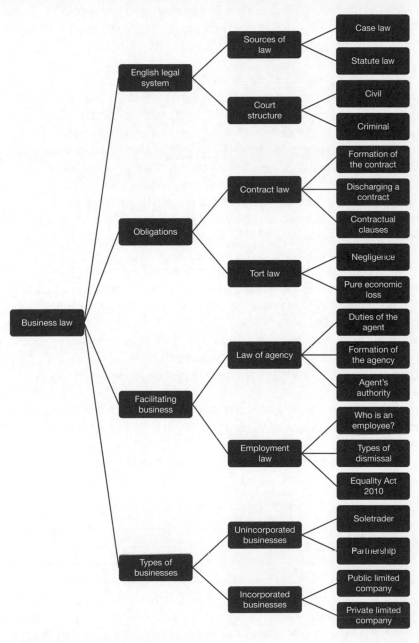

Figure 1.1 Overview of *Beginning Business Law*

Beginning Business Law serves two purposes. The first is to introduce students who are studying on non-law courses to how the law of England and Wales relates to business. The second is to serve as an introduction to business law for law students who are studying this as a distinct module. This book is not intended to be the final word on the different areas of law explored in each chapter. Rather it is intended to introduce you to the key principles and concepts. Each chapter contains an annotated further reading list and each of the textbooks and articles listed there are intended to help you build upon your understanding of the material covered in this book.

Throughout the book there are realistic scenarios and on-the-spot questions that are designed to help you appreciate how the law relates to business transactions. In reality, it is not easy to divide the different areas of law into distinct topics that can be addressed in isolation, as in practice you may encounter an issue that involves the consideration of a number of different areas of law. Imagine that Muneeba, Kingsford and Sonya have set up a business. They manufacture and sell bespoke furniture and employ Rhonson to deliver the furniture to their clients. Rhonson is supplied with a van and while delivering furniture to their clients he crashes into a cyclist, thereby causing the cyclist to break both her legs. Within this scenario there are a number of important issues to consider:

- What type of business did Muneeba, Kingsford and Sonya establish? This is important as, if the business is unincorporated (i.e. a partnership), then they would be personally liable if the business is sued and could end up losing their own personal assets (Chapters 8–10).
- There may be an issue of liability for late delivery of the furniture and other issues arising under the Sale of Goods Act 1979 (Chapters 3 and 4).
- The court may hold that Rhonson has been negligent and therefore he may be liable in tort (Chapter 5).
- The business, or Muneeba, Kingsford and Sonya personally, may be vicariously liable for Rhonson's negligence if the court holds that he is an employee (Chapters 4 and 6).
- Rhonson could be dismissed for gross misconduct and other breaches of his employment contract (Chapter 6).

ANSWERING QUESTIONS

Throughout your study of the law you will be asked by your lecturer to answer both problem questions and essay questions. It is an important skill to be able to look at a set of facts and to provide accurate legal advice that will enable you to write a legal opinion based upon a given scenario. In each chapter of *Beginning Business Law* there are a number of 'on-the-spot questions' and these are designed to test and consolidate your understanding of the law. To assist your comprehension of the material, it is useful to attempt these questions in order to ensure that you have understood the law to which the question relates.

When faced with a problem question you need to be able to first identify the issues, second state the relevant law, third apply the law to the facts and finally provide a conclusion in order to advise the fictional client. It is important that when you are advising a client that your answer is based on the law and not just your own opinion.

USING THE LAW

In Chapter 2 we will look at the different sources of law that you will encounter in your studies. The two that you will use most frequently are case law (or common law) and statute law (Acts of Parliament). It is important that you make reference to the original material rather than just relying on a brief summary from a textbook. We will look at how to access these below.

RESOURCES

There are a number of online resources that can be used for free. These include www.legislation.gov.uk which contains all relevant Acts of Parliament and the British and Irish Legal Information Institute (www.bailii.org) which is a database of important legal cases. You should start to regularly use these resources as this will assist you with your studies.

Your university will subscribe to online legal databases such as *Westlaw* or *Lexis Library*. These will give you access to cases, legislation and a number of different academic and practitioner journals. If you are unsure of whether your university subscribes to these databases you should contact your librarian who can advise you as to this. There are a number of academic and practitioner journals that focus on business law. These journals include the *Journal of Business Law*, the *Company Lawyer* and the *Business Law Review*. You will also find it useful to refer to more general journals such as the *Cambridge Law Journal*, the *Law Quarterly Review* and the *Modern Law Review*. You can access these electronically, although older articles may sometimes only be available in hardcopy.

Chapter 2
The English legal system

LEARNING OBJECTIVES

After reading this chapter, you should be able to:

- appreciate that there are a number of different legal systems in the United Kingdom;
- define the sources of law in the English legal system;
- understand the operation of the court structure and the role served by each court or tribunal;
- comprehend the different rules of statutory interpretation; and
- appreciate the meaning of key terms that will be encountered throughout the rest of this book.

INTRODUCTION

This chapter will provide you with an introduction to the English and Welsh legal system. Although commonly referred to as the *English* legal system, it does in fact also include Wales.

This chapter is intended to help you navigate the different areas of law featured in this book and to provide you with some context as to how the legal system operates. If you are new to law, you will no doubt be experiencing some of the terminology for the first time and, consequently, it is useful to understand what exactly a particular term means. It is also extremely important to appreciate the court structure and to understand how the courts interpret Acts of Parliament. We will briefly consider some important issues as to whether judges make law, could a court declare an Act of Parliament to be invalid if the Act is discriminatory, and what is the domestic courts' relationship with the European Union and the Council of Europe.

THE UNITED KINGDOM'S LEGAL SYSTEMS

The United Kingdom contains a number of different nations which have their own legal systems. The Acts of Union 1707 which joined the Kingdoms of England and Scotland to create Great Britain expressly preserved the two different legal systems. This means that England and Wales, Northern Ireland and Scotland have their own courts and law. We shall see that they share the Supreme Court as the highest appellate court for all civil appeals and, with the exception of Scotland, all criminal appeals.

The United Kingdom's Parliament is based in Westminster and it enacts law in the form of an Act of Parliament. It is important to note that an Act of Parliament may apply across the entire United Kingdom in full or part, i.e. certain provisions may only apply in England and Wales and not in Northern Ireland and Scotland.

Two parliaments and two national assemblies

The previous Labour government which came to power in 1997 devolved power from Westminster and held referendums in Scotland and Wales to ask the people living there whether they wished for power to be devolved. The electorate supported devolving powers and Parliament enacted legislation to achieve this. As a result of the Scotland Act 1998 there is now a Scottish Parliament at Holyrood, which has the power to enact legislation under the powers devolved to it by the United Kingdom's Parliament. The Government of Wales Acts 1998 and 2006 have created the National Assembly of Wales and have given the assembly law making powers. It is important to note that neither legislative body can legislate beyond the powers given to it by Westminster. An example of this was the Agricultural Sector (Wales) Bill that was enacted by the National Assembly of Wales and this bill was referred to the Supreme Court by the Attorney-General, in order to determine whether the bill was within the assembly's legislative competence (*Agricultural Sector (Wales) Bill Reference by the Attorney General for England and Wales* [2014] UKSC 43).

Northern Ireland has its own national assembly which is based at Stormont. It is important to appreciate the United Kingdom is not a federal state. This is unlike the United States of America where the United States' constitution establishes the separation of power between the federal and individual state governments. In the United Kingdom it is up to Parliament as to the degree of power it devolves to regional parliaments or assemblies. However, politically, as opposed to legally, once power has been devolved, it is very difficult to revoke it.

SOURCES OF LAW

Throughout this book you will encounter a number of different sources of law. We will now consider each source of law in turn.

The common law

The common law is otherwise known as case law. Students studying law in a common law jurisdiction, as opposed to a civil law jurisdiction, will appreciate the importance of judicial decisions as a significant source of law.

Development of the common law

The common law is a product of reforms to the legal system by monarchs such as Henry II, who wished to assert royal authority after decades of civil war. The common law courts were based at the Palace of Westminster and included the Court of Common Pleas, the Court of Exchequer and the Court of King's Bench. In addition to hearing cases at Westminster, the judges would travel around the country and dispense justice. These travelling courts were known as the assize.

From the late Middle Ages barristers were trained by the Inns of Court, which still exist in London, and legal education took the shape of mooting and listening to legal arguments. The common law was developed by judges such as Sir Edward Coke in the seventeenth century and Lord Mansfield in the eighteenth century.

Where did equity come from?

You will notice that in Chapter 3 (which explores contract law) we will discuss both common law and equitable remedies. Equity was developed as a solution to the formality and rigidity of the common law. The Lord Chancellor, on behalf of the monarch, would dispense justice where the claimant could not obtain a remedy in one of the common law courts. This led to the development of the Court of Chancery. The common law judges were jealous of the Court of Chancery, and in the *Earl of Oxford's case* (1615) 21 ER 485 it was held that where there was a conflict between common law and equity, equity would prevail. We will see below that the two systems were merged in the late nineteenth century.

Do judges make law?

Historically, much of the law was created by judges and examples of this include tort law and contract law. Some judges have denied that the courts make law as this is seen as usurping the role of Parliament. In *Duport Steels Ltd v Sirs* [1980] 1 WLR 142, Lord Diplock stated that 'Parliament makes the laws, the judiciary interpret them' (at p. 157). However, Lord Reid writing extra-judicially has observed that judges do make law and to say otherwise is a fairy tale (see 'The judge as lawmaker' (1972) 12 *Journal of the Society of Public Teachers of Law* 23). Today the majority of case law will concern statutory interpretation. We will look at the different rules of statutory interpretation below.

Custom

In the past local custom was an important source of law. It is rarely used today.

Acts of Parliament

Parliament enacts primary legislation known as an Act of Parliament. This is statutory law and is the superior law in the United Kingdom. According to the Doctrine of Parliamentary Sovereignty no one, including the courts, may challenge the validity of an Act of Parliament. Furthermore, there are no restrictions on the subject matter that Parliament may legislate on. Parliament could choose to legislate to make it lawful to discriminate on the basis of gender or race. This was a point expressed by Lord Hoffmann in *Secretary of State for the Home Department, Ex Parte Simms* [2000] 2 AC 115:

> Parliamentary sovereignty means that Parliament can, if it chooses, legislate contrary to fundamental principles of human rights . . . The constraints upon its exercise by Parliament are ultimately political, not legal. But the principle of legality means that Parliament must squarely confront what it is doing and accept the political cost.

The United Kingdom's Parliament is bicameral. This means that Parliament is comprised of two Houses of Parliament, which are the House of Commons and the House of Lords. Parliament makes legislation through the powers of the Queen in Parliament and once legislation has been approved by both Houses of Parliament the bill, as it is then known, must receive royal assent in order for it to become an Act.

The people who sit in the House of Commons are known as Members of Parliament (MPs). MPs are directly elected by the people living in constituencies through a method known as first past the post. This means that a candidate who has the most votes, even if they do not enjoy a majority of all the votes cast, will become that constituency's MP.

None of the members of the House of Lords are democratically elected. Its members are comprised of life peers, hereditary peers and Church of England bishops. The vast majority of the hereditary peers were removed by the House of Lords Act 1999. The Coalition government (which was formed from the Conservative and Liberal Democrat parties) planned to reform the House of Lords during the 2010–2015 Parliament. However, the attempt at introducing further reforms to the House of Lords was eventually abandoned.

A bill can be introduced in either House of Parliament. If a bill is introduced into the House of Commons it will receive three readings before being sent up to the House of Lords, where the bill will also receive three readings. The bill will be debated in each House and amendments suggested. If the House of Lords rejects the bill and it is sent back to the

House of Commons, then ultimately the Parliament Acts 1911 and 1949 could be used to bypass the House of Lords and send the bill to receive royal assent. Typically, the two Houses will negotiate and the Lords will suggest amendments and these amendments will be considered by the Commons. This process is known as Ping-Pong, as it demonstrates the interaction between the two Houses.

An Act of Parliament can give a minister or a local authority the power to make laws known as delegated or secondary legislation.

European Union law

The United Kingdom joined the European Union (previously the European Economic Communities) in January 1973. Parliament needed to enact the European Communities Act 1972 in order for the United Kingdom to be able to give effect to its legal obligations as a member of the European Union.

The membership of the European Union is important for businesses for a number of reasons. UK businesses are able to enjoy free movement of goods across all 28 member states, free movement of services, capital and people. The European Union has reduced barriers to trade and has created new opportunities for businesses to take advantage of. There are a number of sources of European Union law, which include regulations, directives, the treaty articles, and the judgments of the Court of Justice of the European Union (CJEU). Individuals and businesses are able to enforce the rights created by European Union law in domestic courts. The CJEU created the principle that European Union law was superior to the laws of the individual member states, where a particular law related to a matter over which the European Union has competence (see *Costa v ENEL* [1964] ECR 585). Much of what we look at in employment law is the result of European Union law (see Chapter 7). Of relevance to businesses are the measures designed to prevent the formation of cartels and the abuse of a dominant position. Large multinational corporations such as Microsoft have been fined by the European Commission, which is the governing body of the European Union, for abusing their dominant position (see *Microsoft Corp v European Commission* (T-167/08) [2012] 5 CMLR 15).

Council of Europe

The United Kingdom was a founding member of the Council of Europe which is the organisation responsible for the European Convention on Human Rights (ECHR). Much of the ECHR was incorporated into domestic law by the Human Rights Act 1998 (HRA 1998). The HRA 1998 was intended to permit individuals or businesses whose human rights had been violated by a public authority to bring their claims in a domestic court, rather than having to lodge an application with the European Court of Human Rights in Strasbourg. It is important to note that a company can be a victim for the purposes of the ECHR (see *Sunday Times v United Kingdom (131666/87)* (1992) 14 EHRR 229). The HRA 1998 was intended to have a vertical effect which meant that claims could only be brought against a public authority (s.6 HRA 1998). In *Aston Cantlow and Wilmcote with Billesley Parochial Church Council v Wallbank* [2004] 1 AC 546, Lord Nicholls stated that there were two types of public authority, core and hybrid. A core public authority would be the police. A hybrid public authority would be a body which carries out a service of a public nature. This means that a business could be regarded as a public authority where it was carrying out a service such as running a prison or an immigration detention centre.

COURT STRUCTURE

It is worth noting that each of the legal systems within the United Kingdom has its own court structure. We are concerned with the court structure for England and Wales. In addition to the courts there are tribunals that are an important part of the legal system and these include employment tribunals. The court structure in England and Wales is complex and this is only intended to introduce you to the courts that you will encounter while studying business law (see Figure 2.1).

As a result of the Constitutional Reform Act 2005, the head of the judiciary in England and Wales is now the Lord Chief Justice. Previously, it had been the Lord Chancellor, who was also a senior member of the government.

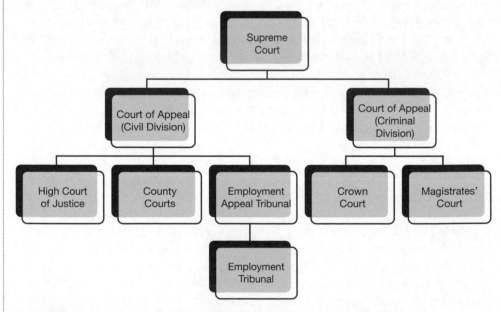

Figure 2.1 Introduction to the court structure in England and Wales

Private law (contract, tort, business disputes)

Depending on the complexity of the issue and the amount of damages sought, a claim in private law will either be heard by the County Court or the High Court.

The High Court

The High Court has a number of specialist courts that will hear different types of disputes. This will enable the judges to specialise and each court is governed by its own rules under the Civil Procedure Rules 1998.

As we saw above, historically the common law and equity were distinct and a claimant could only get an equitable remedy if they brought their case to the Court of Chancery. Two important Acts of Parliament known as the Supreme Court of Judicature Acts 1873 and 1875 merged the two systems into the High Court of Justice. The Acts brought the common law courts and the Court of Chancery together and in addition created a new court known as the Probate, Divorce and Admiralty Division. Importantly, this reform means that both common law and equitable remedies could be awarded by all courts. This is the system that prevails today. Further reforms in 1880 created the Queen's Bench Division of the High Court. This amalgamated the common law courts.

Which division of the High Court will hear your dispute?

Chancery Division – for a claim involving intellectual property, bankruptcy, a business dispute or a claim involving company law. This will be relevant to Chapters 8–10.

Queen's Bench Division – for a claim involving negligence, personal injury, breach of contract and non-payment of a debt. This will be relevant to Chapters 3–5.

Admiralty, Commercial and Mercantile Court – for a claim involving international trade disputes, banking disputes, collision of ships, carriage of cargo and arbitration disputes. This will be relevant to Chapter 4.

Technology and Construction Court – for a claim involving software disputes, engineering disputes and building or construction disputes.

The case will be heard by a judge who will give judgment. There is no jury. Until recently, in defamation cases there was a jury. This can be contrasted with the United States, where popular television programmes regularly feature lawyers in civil trials that involve a jury.

A decision of the High Court can be appealed to the Civil Division of the Court of Appeal. In exceptional circumstances it may be possible to bypass the Court of Appeal and appeal directly to the Supreme Court. This procedure is known as leapfrogging.

Court of Appeal (Civil Division)

The judges who sit in the Court of Appeal are known as Lord Justices of Appeal and three judges will hear an appeal. The court is presided over by the Master of the Rolls and this is a very senior position. It is not uncommon for judges who have been members of the highest appeal court, previously the Appellate Committee of the House of Lords and now the Supreme Court, to return to the Court of Appeal as the Master of the Rolls. The classic example is Lord Denning and more recent examples include Lord Neuberger and Lord Dyson. The Court of Appeal is based in the Royal Courts of Justice and members of the public are able to attend and watch proceedings.

Supreme Court

The Supreme Court was created by the Constitutional Reform Act 2005 and heard its first case in October 2009. It replaced the Appellate Committee of the House of Lords which was based in the Palace of Westminster. The judges were known as Lords of Appeal in Ordinary, or colloquially as Law Lords, and were able to take part in parliamentary debates. This was controversial and many people including a member of the court, Lord Steyn, believed that this undermined the separation of powers. Today, those judges who sit in the Supreme Court are known now as Justices of the Supreme Court. The Supreme Court is the final court to which all civil cases from across the United Kingdom can be appealed. We will see that it is possible to make an application to the European Court of Human Rights in Strasbourg where there is an allegation that there has been a breach of human rights.

Key definition: The separation of powers

This is an important theory which states that the powers of law making, governing the country and determining whether there has been a breach of the law must be carried out by three distinct branches of government.

Criminal law

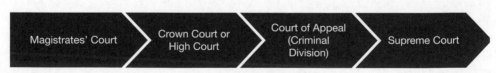

Figure 2.2 When a case is tried at the Magistrates' Court

Figure 2.3 When a case is tried at the Crown Court

All criminal cases start off at the Magistrates' Court and depending on the seriousness of the offence the defendant will either be tried at the Magistrates' Court for minor criminal offences or committed to the Crown Court for more serious offences (see Figures 2.2 and 2.3):

- Indictable only offences (i.e. murder) must be tried in the Crown Court.
- Triable either-way offences (i.e. fraud) can be tried in either the Crown Court or the Magistrates' Court.
- Summary only offences (i.e. battery) must be tried in the Magistrates' Court.

Magistrates' Court

There are two types of magistrates. The first type are lay magistrates who are volunteers and have no legal training. They are assisted by a trained legal advisor who advises the magistrates on the law. The second type are known as District Judges, who are qualified lawyers of at least seven years' practicing experience. Magistrates try over 90 per cent of criminal cases (see 'Court statistics quarterly April to June 2013: Ministry of Justice statistics bulletin', *Ministry of Justice*, 26 September 2013). Appeals against conviction and sentencing decisions will be heard at the Crown Court. It will also be possible to appeal on a point of law by way of case stated to the Queen's Bench Division of the High Court.

Crown Court

At the Crown Court the trial is presided over by a judge. The judge will make decisions as to the law. However, the jury, which is comprised of 12 members of the public, will make the decision as to whether to convict or acquit the defendant. Although juries try only a small minority of all criminal cases, in public consciousness it is the jury that is seen to epitomise the criminal trial. It is possible to appeal against the decision of the Crown Court on a point of law or the sentence imposed to the Criminal Division of the Court of Appeal. It will also be possible to appeal on a point of law by way of case stated to the Queen's Bench Division of the High Court.

Court of Appeal (Criminal Division)

The Criminal Division of the Court of Appeal will hear appeals on points of law and sentencing decisions.

Supreme Court

The Supreme Court will hear appeals from the Court of Appeal. It is the highest domestic court for all criminal appeals from England and Wales, and Northern Ireland. Appeals can only be heard from Scotland where this involves a devolution issue.

Employment law

In the United Kingdom there is a separate tribunal system and there are many different types of specialist tribunals. Recently there have been significant reforms and this has resulted in increased fees for those wishing to bring a claim against their employer.

Employment tribunal

An employee can bring a claim to the employment tribunal and the decision of the employment tribunal can be appealed on a point of law to the Employment Appeal Tribunal.

Employment Appeal Tribunal

The decision can be appealed on a point of law to the Civil Division of the Court of Appeal. Finally, the decision of the Court of Appeal can be appealed to the Supreme Court.

OTHER JURISDICTIONS IN THE UNITED KINGDOM

Northern Ireland

Northern Ireland has its own court structure and both civil and criminal appeals can be heard by the United Kingdom Supreme Court.

Scotland

Only civil appeals and those criminal appeals involving devolution issues may be appealed to the United Kingdom Supreme Court.

OTHER COURTS

Court of Justice of the European Union

Key definition: Court of Justice of the European Union

The superior court of the European Union.

Key definition: European Court of Human Rights

The court that determines whether there has been a violation of the European Convention on Human Rights by a contracting state.

The Court of Justice of the European Union (CJEU) is the court that is tasked with ensuring compliance with European Union law and providing the authoritative interpretation of EU law. It is based in Luxemburg and its judges represent each of the member states. If there is an issue relating to the interpretation of EU law the domestic court can make a preliminary reference to the CJEU under Article 267 TFEU.

Confusingly, the court used to be known as the European Court of Justice and some commentators referred to it as Luxemburg, which refers to where the court is based. Somewhat confusingly, in light of the paragraph below, the court might be referred to by media as the European Court.

European Court of Human Rights

The European Court of Human Rights (ECtHR) is based in Strasbourg and individuals and businesses can bring claims against their own country where there as an allegation that there has been a violation of the European Convention on Human Rights (ECHR). The ECtHR cannot overrule a judgment of a domestic court such as the United Kingdom Supreme Court. However, it can impose a monetary fine on the United Kingdom, but it has no power to enforce this. The decisions of the ECtHR are an important source of law as under s.2(1) of the HRA 1998 the domestic courts must take these into account. It has been the practice of the House of Lords and Supreme Court to choose to follow the decisions of the ECtHR as to the interpretation and extent of the ECHR (see the approach of Lord Bingham in *R (Ullah) v Special Adjudicator* [2004] 2 AC 323).

Privy Council

The Judicial Committee of the Privy Council hears appeals from those countries where this court is still the highest court of appeal. The number of countries to use the Privy Council is decreasing. New Zealand only finally abolished the right to appeal a case to the Privy Council in 2004, with the New Zealand Supreme Court having been established by the Supreme Court Act 2003. Decisions of the Privy Council are persuasive as a legal authority, and thus while not binding on English and Welsh courts, the Privy Council's decisions are very influential. One example of this is the case of *Attorney General for Jersey v Holley* [2005] UKPC 23 which was heard by nine Lords of Appeal in Ordinary and reconsidered the partial defence of provocation for murder. Throughout this book you will see how decisions of the Privy Council have shaped the law.

COMPOSITION OF THE JUDICIARY

The judiciary is perceived as being out of touch with normal people and is characterised as white, upper class and male. The composition of the judiciary is being addressed by the body responsible for the appointment of judges, the Judicial Appointments Commission, and there have been calls to introduce a quota system to ensure that there is more diversity. The Deputy President of the Supreme Court, Baroness Hale of Richmond, who is the only female Justice of the Supreme Court, has highlighted the need for greater diversity.

On-the-spot question

Newbury Ltd and Duxford Ltd enter into a contract, whereby Newbury Ltd agrees to sell 4,000 sofas to Duxford Ltd in return for £1,200,000. When the sofas are delivered to Duxford Ltd's premise they are found to be water damaged. Duxford Ltd wishes to sue Newbury Ltd for breach of contract.

Sonya works for Bill who is a sole trader. Last Monday Bill summoned Sonya to his office and said that she was no longer needed and that as of today she no longer works for him. Sonya was given no notice that she was going to be dismissed and argues that the dismissal was for an unfair reason.

The Morning Headline is a national newspaper and its website has been shut down as a result of Parliament enacting the Press Regulation Act (fictitious), which was introduced in order to control the press. *The Morning Headline* is alleging that its right under Article 10 of the ECHR to freedom of expression has been violated. Last week the Supreme Court has ruled that the Press Regulation Act (fictitious) cannot be challenged as it is an Act of Parliament. *The Morning Headline* wishes to appeal.

Which of the courts that we have discussed above would hear the claims brought by Duxford Ltd, Sonya and *The Morning Headline*?

STATUTORY INTERPRETATION

The role of court is to interpret Acts of Parliament. It is essential that the courts do this in order to apply the law as Parliament intended. There are a number of rules of statutory interpretation. The literal rule is where a court will read the Act and apply it in accordance with the ordinary meaning of the words used in the statute. A well-drafted Act of Parliament should be capable of being read and interpreted clearly. However, there will be times where the literal rule will not be of much assistance. This will be the case where the literal interpretation of the statutory provision will produce a result that would be considered absurd or inconsistent with the intention of Parliament. This would be where a statutory provision has been poorly drafted or the provision, even if clearly drafted, would lead to an absurd result that Parliament would never have intended. If this occurs, then the courts will use the golden rule. The mischief rule is used to remedy a badly drafted statutory provision and to give the statute the effect that Parliament had intended. Therefore, the courts will read the statutory provision in light of what Parliament had intended (see *Inco Europe v First Choice Distribution* [2000] WLR 586).

Since the decision of the House of Lords in *Pepper v Hart* [1993] AC 593, the courts have been able to refer to *Hansard*, which is the record of parliamentary proceedings, in order to ascertain what Parliament's intention was when enacting a bill. *Hansard* is used where the statutory provision is 'ambiguous or obscure or leads to an absurdity'. The statement relied upon in *Hansard* must be clear and needs to have been delivered by a minister or a promoter of the bill.

DOCTRINE OF PRECEDENT

In English and Welsh law there is a hierarchy of courts and the courts use a doctrine of precedent to determine which decisions are binding upon them. Decisions of the Supreme Court (previously the House of Lords) are binding on all lower courts. Likewise, decisions of the Court of Appeal are binding on all lower courts. This means that a court is bound by decisions made by a higher court and must follow that court's decision, unless it is possible to distinguish this decision on the facts before it. The *Practice Statement (HL: Judicial*

Precedent) [1966] 1 WLR 1234 stated that the House of Lords was not bound by its own previous decisions. This applies now to the Supreme Court. The Court of Appeal is bound by its own previous decisions unless it can rely upon an exception (see *Young v Bristol Aeroplane Co.* [1944] KB 718).

RATIO DECIDENDI AND *OBITER DICTA*

The actual decision in a case forms the *ratio decidendi* and it is this that is binding on lower courts. Imagine that the Supreme Court in *Monday v Tuesday (fictitious)* held that in circumstance X no damages were obtainable. The case was heard by five judges. This decision was reached by four judges who all agreed that in circumstance X no damages were obtainable. These four judges formed the majority, and it is their judgment that is binding. Each judge in the majority gave an individual judgment and spoke at length about the different circumstances where compensation might be obtainable. This would be *obiter dicta* as this was a by the way comment and would be useful in the future should one of these listed circumstances arise in the future. However, even then it would not be the *ratio decidendi*. However, in our scenario one of the judges disagreed with the majority, and in her dissenting judgment she argued that damages should be obtainable. This is known as a dissenting opinion and would be *obiter dicta*. Judicial dissent is important as it allows for an alternative approach to the law and judicial dissents have resulted in changes to the law, especially if the dissenting judge was a member of the Court of Appeal, and upon appeal the dissent is preferred to decision reached by the majority. An example of this is the House of Lords' decision in *Gibson v Manchester City Council* [1979] 1 WLR 294, where their Lordships preferred the dissenting opinion in the Court of Appeal to the decision reached by the majority (for an interesting discussion on judicial dissent see Lord Kerr, 'Dissenting judgments – self indulgence or self sacrifice?', available at http://supremecourt.uk/docs/speech-121008.pdf).

LEGAL PROFESSION

The most common routes to becoming a lawyer are to undertake a law degree known as a LLB, to complete the Graduate Diploma in Law after studying a non-law degree or to train with ILEX. It is possible for a student who has studied a business degree to undertake the Graduate Diploma in Law and then study on the same professional training courses as LLB students.

Students wishing to train as solicitors must undertake the Legal Practice Course and then complete a two-year training contract, whereas students who wish to train as a barrister must undertake the Bar Professional Training Course and then complete a one year pupillage.

In England and Wales there is a distinction between solicitors and barristers. Historically, barristers represented clients in court and were instructed by solicitors who provided all other legal services. In many countries there is no longer this distinction. Students studying on the Bar Professional Training Course must be members of one of the four Inns of Court, which are Middle Temple, Inner Temple, Lincoln's Inn and Gray's Inn. Practising barristers must also be members of the Bar Council and the profession is regulated by the Bar Standards Board. Solicitors are members of the Law Society and the profession is regulated by the Solicitors Regulation Authority.

Key definition: Claimant

The person who is bringing a claim in civil law is known as the claimant. Previously, such a person was known as a plaintiff.

Key definition: Defendant

The person who is defending the claim in civil law or who is accused of having committed a criminal offence is known as the defendant.

Key definition: Victim

The person who has made an allegation that the defendant has breached the criminal law and that they have suffered as a result is known as the victim.

Key definition: Prosecution

The Crown Prosecution Service (CPS) brings most criminal prosecutions. The CPS was established in 1986 as a result of the Prosecution of Offences Act 1985. Prior to this a prosecution would be brought by the police force where the offence was committed. There are other bodies in the United Kingdom that have powers to prosecute, such as the RSPCA.

SUMMARY

- There are a number of different sources of law in the English legal system.
- There is a different court structure for civil and criminal law.
- The courts use a number of different rules to interpret Acts of Parliament.
- It is important to distinguish between *ratio decidendi* and *obiter dicta.*
- The legal profession distinguishes between solicitors and barristers.

FURTHER READING

Berlins, M. and Dyer, C. *The Law Machine*, 5th edn (Penguin, 2000) – this is a very succinct and highly readable introduction to the English legal system and the legal profession.

Darbyshire, P. *Darbyshire on the English Legal System*, 10th edn (Sweet & Maxwell, 2011) – refer to this book for an authoritative and highly readable account of the English legal system.

Lord Kerr, 'Dissenting judgments – self indulgence or self sacrifice?' *The Birkenhead Lecture*, 8 October 2012, available at http://supremecourt.uk/docs/speech-121008.pdf) – refer to this lecture for a judicial perspective on the role of dissenting judgments.

Slapper, G. *How the Law Works*, 3rd edn (Routledge, 2013) – refer to this book for an accessible introduction to the English legal system.

Slapper, G. and Kelly, D. *The English Legal System*, 16th edn (Routledge, 2015) – this is an extremely authoritative and comprehensive account of the English legal system.

Chapter 3
Contract law

LEARNING OBJECTIVES

After reading this chapter, you should be able to:

- appreciate the requirements that are needed in order to have a legally enforceable contract;
- understand the consequences for the contracting parties where there is misrepresentation, mistake, duress, illegality and undue influence;
- comprehend how a contract can be discharged by performance, acceptance, breach and frustration;
- demonstrate an awareness of the remedies that are available where a contract has been breached.

Every business transaction will involve the use of a contract. Without a contract, a business agreement will not be legally enforceable. This chapter is intended as an introduction to the law of contract. It is essential that you understand the key concepts covered in this chapter. To demonstrate how the law applies in practice we will consider how the law relates to transactions entered into by Snow Ltd. Snow Ltd is based in York and specialises in building loft extensions. Imagine that Snow Ltd wishes to contract with Murphy Ltd, in which case the contract could be written or verbal. Both written and verbal contracts are equally valid. However, in an event of a dispute, it will be easier to prove the terms of the contract if the contract is written. When advising Snow Ltd this would be a point that you would make; alternatively, if you were a director of Snow Ltd, you would appreciate the advantages of recording the terms of the contract in writing.

In this chapter we will look at the requirements for a legally enforceable contract, the factors that could make the contract invalid, the way the terms of the contract are classified, how a contract can be discharged, and finally the remedies for breach of contract.

FIVE REQUIREMENTS FOR A LEGALLY ENFORCEABLE CONTRACT

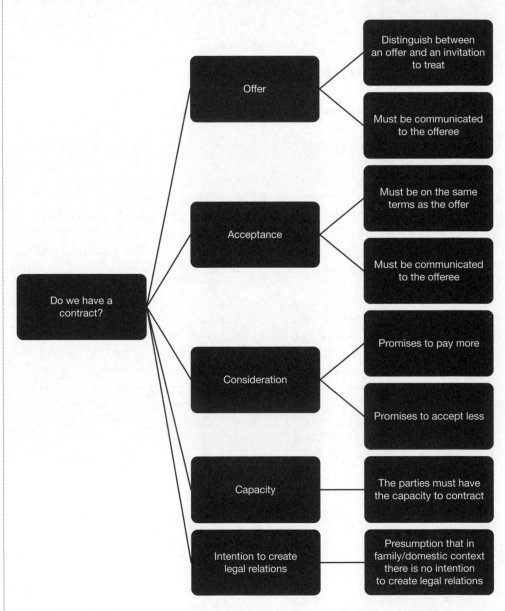

Figure 3.1 Requirements needed to create a legally enforceable contract

Offer

> **Key definition: Offeror**
>
> The offeror is the person who is making the offer.
>
> **Key definition: Offeree**
>
> The offeree is the person to whom the offer is made and who can choose whether to accept it.
>
> **Key definition: Bilateral contract**
>
> This is where an offer (promise) is made in return for a promise, i.e. 'I will give you £50 in return for your mobile phone'.
>
> **Key definition: Unilateral contract**
>
> This is where an offer (promise) is made for the requested action to be performed by anyone who the offer is communicated to, i.e. a poster on a tree that states that 'I have lost my cat and will give you £50 if you find her'.

The person making the offer is known as the offeror. The person to whom the offer is made is known as the offeree. The offeror can make a bilateral offer, which is an offer to a specific individual in return for a promise, or a unilateral offer, which is an offer made to the world in return for an act to be performed. The offer must be clear and precise and capable of being accepted. Any ambiguity will invalidate the offer as therefore it is incapable of being objectively understood. This makes sense, as how could you possibly accept an offer that was capable of multiple meanings and could not be objectively defined. The offer needs to be communicated to the offeree. Once the offer is made to the offeree it can be revoked by the offeror at any time before there is acceptance. The notice of revocation must actually be communicated to the offeree before it can become effective.

It is important to distinguish between offers and invitations to treat. An invitation to treat is where someone indicates a willingness to enter into a business transaction, but in doing this they are not making an offer that can be accepted. Rather, the offer will be made at a later time. Examples of invitations to treat include adverts, the display of goods in shops, the display of goods in a shop window and goods advertised on a website. The distinction between an offer and an invitation to treat is important for a number of reasons. First, if we look at the decision in *Fisher v Bell* [1961] 1 QB 394, in that case the display of a flick-knife in a shop window was held to amount to an invitation to treat. This was fortunate for the shop owner, as it was a criminal offence to offer such a knife for sale. In *Pharmaceutical Society of Great Britain v Boots Cash Chemist (Southern) Ltd* [1953] 1 QB 401 the court held that the display of goods in the shop amounted to an invitation to treat. In this case had it been held by the court to amount to an offer, then the shop would have committed an offence, as it was illegal to offer up the goods for sale. Second, there is a concern that if adverts were generally treated as offers, then the offeror might face a situation where she is unable to meet the orders placed by all of the offerees.

However, it is possible for an advert to amount to an offer. This will be the case where the advert requires the performance of an act, such as providing the required information (see *Williams v Carwardine* [1833] 4 B & Ad 621). So long as the offer is sufficiently clear and precise, and is capable of being accepted, then the advert will amount to an offer. An example of this is *Carlill v Carbolic Smoke Ball Co* [1893] 1 QB 256.

KEY CASE ANALYSIS: *Carlill v Carbolic Smoke Ball Co* [1893] 1 QB 256

Background

Carbolic Smoke Ball Co manufactured a product that was advertised as preventing a user from catching influenza. The company promised that anyone who used its product in the way that it prescribed and still caught influenza would receive £100. The advert informed potential customers that the Carbolic Smoke Ball Co had set aside funds at a bank to cover any payments.

Principle established

The Court of Appeal held that due to an advert offering £100 to anyone who purchased the defendant's product and used it in the prescribed manner, the customer would be legally entitled to recover the money in the event that they caught influenza. The Court of Appeal held that the advert amounted to a unilateral contract and the offer had been made to the whole world. It was sufficiently precise and the assurance that there was £1,000 held at a bank demonstrated an intention to be bound. Despite the Carbolic Smoke Ball Co's arguments, the advert was a mere puff, and not an offer, regardless of the fact that it had been made to such a wide audience.

On-the-spot question

Do you think that the decision in *Carlill v Carbolic Smoke Ball Co* [1893] is correct? What would have happened if 50,000 customers had accepted the offer by using the product and all caught influenza?

Acceptance

The offeree's acceptance must mirror the precise terms of the offer. If the offeree varies the terms of the offer then this will be treated as a counter offer and the original offer will no longer exist (*Hyde v Wrench* (1840) 49 ER 132). This means that the offeree will no longer be able to accept the original offer. However, if the offeree is merely asking whether the offeror would be willing to vary the terms, then this will be regarded as a request for further information and will not invalidate the original offer.

Acceptance must be communicated to the offeror before it is effective. This means that notice of the acceptance must reach the offeror (*Entores Ltd v Miles Far East Corp* [1955] 2 QB 327). Otherwise, how would the offeror know that her offer had been accepted? If the offeror specifies a particular mode of acceptance and the offeree communicates her acceptance via a different mode, then according to *Manchester Diocesan Council of Education v Commercial & General Investments Ltd* [1970] 1 WLR 241, the acceptance will be effective unless the offeror expressly ruled out other forms of communication and the offeree's chosen method of acceptance is no less advantageous to the offeror.

Example

Therefore, if Snow Ltd had offered to build Mrs Haralambous a loft extension for £30,000 and had given Mrs Haralambous seven days to accept its offer, it would be possible for Snow Ltd to revoke its offer any time up until Mrs Haralambous accepts it. However, if Mrs Haralambous informs Snow Ltd of her acceptance, then it is no longer possible for Snow Ltd to revoke the offer.

There are two exceptions to the rule that notice of acceptance must reach the offeror. The first exception is where there is a unilateral offer, such as occurred in *Carlill*. The offeror in *Carlill* was held by the Court of Appeal to have waived the need for the offeree's acceptance to be communicated to the company. The performance of the requested act amounted to acceptance. The second exception is where the acceptance is sent by post. The postal rule states that acceptance takes place when the letter is posted and not when it is actually received by the offeror (*Adams v Lindsell* (1818) 1 B & Ald 681). The postal rule applies even when the letter is lost in the post and is never received by the offeror. Once the letter is posted it is no longer possible for the offeror to revoke her offer. However, you should note that the postal rule will not apply where the letter had been sent to the wrong address (*Korbetis v Transgrain Shipping BV* [2005] EWHC 1345 (QB)). The postal rule only applies to non-instantaneous forms of communication and not to instantaneous communication such as telex (*Entores Ltd* and *Brinkibon v Stahag Stahl und Staglwarenhandels GmbH* [1983] 2 AC 34), text messages or email (see Figure 3.2).

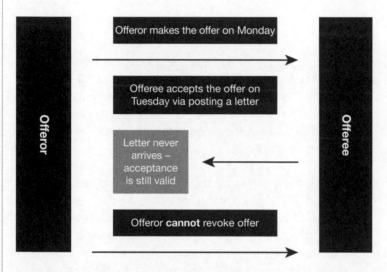

Figure 3.2 The postal rule in operation

There must be an offer that can be accepted

and reversed the policy of selling council houses. The Court of Appeal in *Gibson v Manchester City Council* [1978] 1 WLR 520 held that the conduct of the parties and the correspondence had created a contract. Lord Denning MR had rejected the approach of looking for a clear offer that contained all the finalised terms which only then was capable of being accepted. His Lordship had argued that the court should 'look at the correspondence as a whole and at the conduct of the parties and see therefrom whether the parties have come to an agreement on everything that was material' (at p. 523). The Court of Appeal awarded the remedy of specific performance, which meant that the council had to sell the house to Mr Gibson. The council appealed to the House of Lords.

Principle established

The House of Lords overruled the Court of Appeal's decision and held that there was no contract. The council had never made an offer that was capable of being accepted in the course of the correspondence between it and Mr Gibson and, subsequently, there could be no acceptance by Mr Gibson. The House of Lords rejected the Court of Appeal's approach and held that the conventional method must be adopted in determining whether there had been a contract. Lord Diplock held that:

> I can see no reason in the instant case for departing from the conventional approach of looking at the handful of documents relied upon as constituting the contract sued upon and seeing whether upon their true construction there is to be found in them a contractual offer by the corporation to sell the house to Mr Gibson and an acceptance of that offer by Mr Gibson. I venture to think that it was by departing from this conventional approach that the majority of the Court of Appeal was led into error. (at p. 297)

On-the-spot question

Do you prefer the approach of the Court of Appeal or the House of Lords in *Gibson v Manchester City Council*?

Consideration

> **Key definition: Promisor**
>
> The person who is promising to do or to provide something.
>
> **Key definition: Promisee**
>
> The person who wishes to enforce the promise and must provide consideration in return for the promised act.

In order to have a valid contract there needs to be consideration. Before we look at the legal definition of consideration, let us consider how it works in practice. Imagine that Snow Ltd and Mrs Haralambous had agreed that Snow Ltd will build Mrs Haralambous' loft extension for £27,000. However, due to miscalculating the costs of materials, Snow Ltd now informs Mrs Haralambous that she will need to pay an additional £9,000 in order for Snow Ltd to complete the loft extension. Mrs Haralambous agrees to pay the additional £9,000. It is important to consider whether there is a legally enforceable contract for the £27,000 and for the £9,000? In order to answer this question we will have to look at the legal definition of consideration.

Where the promisor has made a promise, the promisee must provide something in return in order to enforce the promise. Otherwise, the promisor has promised you a gift that will be unenforceable should they renege on their promise, such as where a sibling promises to buy you a ticket for a concert for your birthday and later reneges on their promise. You might now be thinking whether such a promise should or should not be enforceable, but while there might be a moral obligation to honour the promise, it should be remembered that we are concerned with whether there is a legal obligation.

Consideration can be defined as the price for which the promise is bought. In *Currie v Misa* (1874–75) LR 10 Ex 153 at 162, Lush J stated that '[a] valuable consideration, in the sense of the law, may consist either in some right, interest, profit, or benefit accruing to the one party, or some forbearance, detriment, loss, or responsibility, given, suffered, or undertaken by the other'. We can see that consideration needs to be something of value in the eyes of the law. This could be monetary or where the promise is refraining from doing something that she has a legal right to do. Consideration need not be adequate; however, it must be sufficient. If Henry were to offer George his computer for £1, then Henry cannot complain when George presents £1 and demands the computer (see *Chappell & Co Ltd v Nestle Co Ltd* [1960] AC 87). The £1 is hardly adequate, yet it is sufficient in the eyes of the law.

Past consideration

In order to enforce the promise, the promisee must have provided consideration. If an act is performed without the promise of payment in return, a subsequent promise of payment will not be enforceable, as the earlier act occurred prior to the promise having been made. Therefore, no consideration has been given in return for the promise to pay, as the earlier act will be insufficient as it amounts to past consideration. It is important to note that there is an exception known as implied assumpsit, which if it applies could make the promise to pay enforceable. However, this will only be the case if, when the act was performed, both parties had appreciated that it was not being informed for free (see *Pao On v Lau Yiu Long* [1980] AC 614).

Existing legal duties

The performance of a legal duty will not amount to good consideration (*Collins v Godefroy* (1831) 1 B & Ad 950). This is because the promisee must perform this legal duty regardless of the promisor's request.

Promises to pay more than originally agreed

Therefore, looking in the example above, Snow Ltd has promised to build the loft extension and Mrs Haralambous is in return promising to pay £27,000. If Mrs Haralambous refused to pay the £27,000, then Snow Ltd could enforce the contract as they have provided consideration by agreeing to build the loft extension. However, what about the additional £9,000? Mrs Haralambous has agreed to pay this money. It would appear that Mrs Haralambous is not receiving anything in exchange from Snow Ltd. The construction of the loft extension is an existing obligation, and so agreeing to perform this contractual obligation in return for additional money will not amount to good consideration (*Stilk v Myrick* (1809) 170 ER 1168). It would appear that if Mrs Haralambous refuses to pay the additional £9,000, Snow Ltd would not be able to sue her for the money, as it has not provided consideration.

We can see that difficulties arise where there is a promise to pay more. According to *Stilk v Myrick*, a promise to pay more is not legally enforceable if the person seeking to enforce the promise has not provided any consideration in return for the additional money. However, the Court of Appeal in *Williams v Roffey Bros & Nicholls (Contractors) Ltd* [1990] 2 WLR 1153 held that a promise to pay more could be enforceable where the party seeking to enforce the additional payment has undertaken to perform the existing contractual obligation and provided the promisor with a practical benefit.

KEY CASE ANALYSIS: *Williams v Roffey Bros & Nicholls (Contractors) Ltd* [1990] 2 WLR 1153

Background

The defendant had the main contract to refurbish a block of flats and late completion of the development would result in the defendant incurring a penalty. The defendant entered into a contract with the claimant who was a subcontractor and would provide carpentry services. Later on the claimant informed the defendant that it could not perform its contractual obligations as it had undercharged when quoting on the contract. The defendant agreed to pay additional money to the claimant and the parties agreed to proceed on this basis. Subsequently, the defendant refused to pay the additional sum and the claimant sought to recover the money.

Principle established

The Court of Appeal held that the claimant could recover the additional money as by continuing to perform his contractual obligations he had prevented the defendant from being penalised for late completion; he had also agreed to a new method of working and had prevented the defendant from having to find new carpenters. This amounted to a practical benefit and therefore the claimant had provided consideration and the promise to pay additional money was legally enforceable.

Snow Ltd might be able to recover the additional £9,000 from Mrs Haralambous only if they could persuade a court that it has provided a practical benefit. A party will not be able to rely on *Williams v Roffey Bros & Nicholls (Contractors) Ltd* where the request amounts to economic duress. We will look at economic duress in more detail below.

Promises to accept less

Imagine that Snow Ltd has built a loft extension for Mr Jones for £24,000. Mr Jones was made redundant from work and now cannot afford to pay the full amount. If Mr Jones informs Snow Ltd that he could only afford to pay £15,000 and Snow Ltd promises to accept this as full payment, then this would amount to a promise to accept less. At a later date could Mr Jones prevent Snow Ltd from seeking to recover the additional £9,000? As a matter of law the answer would be no, as Mr Jones has not provided any consideration to support Snow Ltd's promise to accept less. The leading House of Lords authority is *Foakes v Beer* (1884) 9 App Cas 605, where a promise to accept less was held to be unenforceable as no additional consideration had been provided. If, however, the debtor were to provide something of value in the eyes of the law in exchange for the promise, then that would amount to consideration (see *Pinnell's Case* (1601) 77 ER 237). Mr Jones would be unable to rely upon the argument that his prompt payment might amount to a practical benefit, as in *Re Selectmove Ltd* [1995] 1 WLR 474 it was held by the Court of Appeal that this did not apply to promises to accept less.

Promissory estoppel

Equity is there to provide assistance when the law proves inadequate. We have seen that in law a promise to pay less will not amount to good consideration. However, in equity a promise to accept less could be used as a defence where the promisor who has agreed to accept less is now seeking to recover the full amount. In *Central London Property Trust Ltd v High Trees House Ltd* [1947] KB 130, Denning J revived promissory estoppel and held that this could estop, or prevent, a person from seeking to recover money during the period that reduced payments were made. For example, if you contract to hire a car for 52 weeks and subsequently due to having been made redundant you cannot afford to pay the £250 a week that you had originally agreed to pay, and the other party agrees to accept a lesser amount during the period that you are looking for work, then you would have a defence in equity, should the other attempt to recover the waived amount.

Denning LJ defined the requirements of promissory estoppel in *Combe v Combe* [1951] 2 KB 215 and was clear that it did not give rise to a cause of action 'where none existed before. It only prevents a party from insisting upon his strict legal rights, when it would be unjust to allow him to enforce them, having regard to the dealings which have taken place between the parties' (at p. 219). It was designed to act as a shield to protect a party from being sued for failing to comply with the terms of the original agreement.

Capacity

The fourth requirement needed for there to be a legally enforceable contract is that both parties to the contract must have the capacity to contract. Children, those who are mentally incapacitated and those who are intoxicated do not have the capacity to contract. However, s.3(2) of the Sale of Goods Act 1979 states that where a person without capacity purchases goods then he must pay a reasonable price for them.

Intention to create legal relations

The final requirement is that the parties to a contract must intend to create legal relations. In *Balfour v Balfour* [1919] 2 KB 571 the court held that there was a presumption that where a married couple enter into an agreement they do not intend to make a legally enforceable contract. This applies to other agreements made in a domestic or family setting. Conversely, there is a presumption that in a commercial agreement there is an intention to create legal relations. Both presumptions can be rebutted.

On-the-spot question

? Sarah, Snow Ltd's managing director, has the authority to enter contracts on behalf of Snow Ltd. Sarah is at a trade conference and has just delivered a paper on modern business practice; as her paper went well, she decides to drink several large glasses of wine to celebrate. After finishing the wine Sarah bumps into the manager of a timber supplier who has a trade stand at the conference, and she agrees to purchase £189,000 worth of timber on Snow Ltd's behalf.

Discuss whether there is a legally binding contract.

VITIATING FACTORS

Key definition: Void

Where a contract is void it is treated as if it never existed.

Key definition: Voidable

Where a contract is voidable it will continue to exist unless the innocent party is able to persuade the court to set the contract aside.

A contract can be invalid where there is a vitiating factor present. It is important to note that depending on which factor is present the contract could be void, which is treated as if it never existed, or voidable, which means that the party seeking to set the contract aside must ask the court to avoid the contract. The court does not have to do this.

Misrepresentation

A contract will be voidable where there has been a misrepresentation. The courts have the discretion to award the equitable remedy of rescission, which will avoid the contract.

In order to have an actionable misrepresentation there needs to be a false statement of fact or law. A trade or mere puff is not actionable as it is vague and does not amount to a fact. Generally, a statement of opinion is not actionable (*Bisset v Wilkinson* [1927] AC 177). However, if the maker of the statement of opinion is sufficiently knowledgeable then it could amount to a statement of fact (*Esso Petroleum Co Ltd v Mardon* [1976] QB 801). The statement must be material and have induced the claimant to enter into the contract. The statement need not have been the sole inducement. In *JEB Fasteners Ltd v Mark Bloom & Co* [1983] 1 All ER 583 Stephenson LJ observed:

> [So] long as a misrepresentation plays a real and substantial part, though not by itself a decisive part, in inducing a plaintiff to act, it is a cause of his loss and he relies on it, no matter how strong or how many are the other matters which play their part in inducing him to act.

There are three types of misrepresentation: fraudulent, negligent and innocent. In order to establish that there is a fraudulent misrepresentation the claimant needs to prove that the defendant's statement was fraudulent. The tort of deceit, or fraud, is explored in Chapter 5 and the requirements needed to establish liability for deceit were reiterated in *Derry v Peek* [1899] 14 App Cas 337). The advantage of establishing fraud is that the measure of damages available is greater than for negligence, as there is no need to establish remoteness and it does not matter if the defendant could not have foreseen the claimant's consequential losses (*Doyle v Olby (Ironmongers) Ltd* [1969] 2 QB 158). In tort law the defendant will be liable for negligent statements under the tort of negligent misstatement, which was established in *Hedley Byrne & Co Ltd v Heller & Partners Ltd* [1964] AC 465. However, the Misrepresentation Act 1967 (MA 1967) provides an improvement on the cause of action available in tort, as where there is an alleged negligent misrepresentation, the claimant does not have the burden of proof of establishing that the statement was negligent, as it is the defendant that must prove 'that he had reasonable ground to believe and did believe up to the time the contract was made the facts represented were true' (s.2(2)). Additionally, the measure of damages are the same as for fraud (*Royscot Trust Ltd v Rogerson* [1991] 3 WLR 57 and s.2(1) MA 1967).

The claimant may wish to rescind the contract. We must remember that rescission is an equitable remedy and therefore it is awarded at the discretion of the court. Rescission will not be awarded where one of the four bars is present: lapse of time, the impossibility of returning the parties to their original positions, affirmation by the claimant and third party rights.

Mistake

If there has been a mistake when contracting, then depending on the type of mistake that is present, the contract could be void or voidable. Where there is common mistake the contract is void. There needs to be a fundamental mistake such as the non-existence of the subject matter of the contract. If one of the parties is aware that the other party is mistaken as to the other party's identity, or the terms of the contract, then this will amount to unilateral mistake. This happens when a rogue pretends to be someone else and the other party believes that they are contracting not with the rogue, but rather with the assumed alias. With unilateral mistake the courts have drawn a distinction between where the parties contract on a face to face basis, and when they have contracted at a distance. Where the negotiations have taken place at a distance there will be no contract between the parties; this is because the mistaken party had believed that they were contracting with the assumed alias. On the other hand, when you contract on a face to face basis the law that holds your intention is to contract with the person before you (see *Shogun Finance v Hudson* [2004] 1 AC 919).

Illegality

Illegality is a vitiating factor and a contract could be void if the subject matter of the contract was illegal.

Duress

Imagine that Snow Ltd is owned by two shareholders, Jonathan and Robbie who each have a 50 per cent shareholding. Robbie wishes to purchase Jonathan's shares and as Jonathan is reluctant to sell, Robbie threatens to ensure that Jonathan will not live to enjoy the shares if he does not sell them. Jonathan has been physically threatened and decides to sell the shares to Robbie. Here Robbie has applied physical duress to Jonathan whose consent has been coerced so that his free will has been overborn by the threats. Jonathan could attempt to have the contract avoided as duress makes the contract voidable. This scenario is similar to the case of *Barton v Armstrong* [1976] AC 104. However, it is possible for duress to be economic in nature rather than just physical. The problem with establishing that there has been economic duress is that businesses often try to negotiate from a position of strength and therefore are keen to exploit the other party's weaknesses. This means that the court must distinguish between legitimate commercial pressure and economic duress (*Atlas Express Ltd v Kafco (Importers and Distributors) Ltd* [1989] QB 833). The requirements for establishing economic duress were reiterated by Dyson J in *DSND Subsea Ltd v Petroleum Geo Services ASA* [2000] BLR 530. Dyson J held that there must be illegitimate pressure and that the innocent party had no practical choice, and that this pressure was a significant cause as to why he entered into the contract.

On-the-spot question

? Snow Ltd requires two tons of roof tiles for use on their 146 current loft extensions. Kennington Ltd has a contract with Snow Ltd to supply the tiles and informs Snow Ltd that unless they agree to enter into a contract to buy another two tons of roof tiles, then Kennington Ltd may be unable to fulfil the current contract. Snow Ltd reluctantly enters into the additional contract as they will be unable to find an alternative supplier to meet their existing customer deadlines.

Discuss.

Undue influence

Where one of the parties to the contract unduly influences the other party as a consequence of the relationship that exists between them, then this will make the contract voidable. There will be actual undue influence where there is evidence that it occurred, and there will be presumed undue influence either because of the nature of the parties' relationship, or if on the facts there is a presumption that influence has been exerted. The key cases that have considered the different categories of undue influence have arisen from where a spouse agrees to allow their partner to borrow money from a bank and to use the family home as security (see *Royal Bank of Scotland v Etridge (No 2)* [2001] 4 All ER 449).

PRIVITY OF CONTRACT: WHO CAN ENFORCE THE CONTRACT?

At common law only those who are parties to the contract are able to enforce the terms of the contract (*Tweddle v Atkinson* (1861) 1 B & S 393). This makes sense as the parties are agreeing to enter into a contract and will be bound to honour the terms that they both have agreed. However, the doctrine of privity of contract has historically caused hardship to a third party (especially if the contract was entered into to confer a benefit upon the third party) and a number of exceptions were created. One exception is the undisclosed principal, which we will explore in Chapter 6. This permits an agent to enter into a contract on the principal's behalf and at a later date the principal, whose existence is unknown to the other party, can choose to intervene and enforce the terms of the contract. Another exception is assignment. Assignment is where the parties are able to assign their contractual obligations to third parties.

These are not the only exceptions that exist. A broader exception is the Contracts (Rights of Third Parties) Act 1999, which confers the third parties with the right to enforce the terms of a contract to which they are not a party. The Act stipulates that third parties may have rights where the court refers to them by name, by class or where they match a particular description (s.1(3)). It is important to note that the Act does not confer liability on third parties; rather it just confers the right to enforce a benefit. In Chapter 4 we shall see how it is usual for contracting parties to include a contractual clause that prevents the Act from applying to a particular contract.

EXPRESS OR IMPLIED TERMS

Key definition: Express term

This is a term that the parties have agreed should be included in their contract.

Key definition: Implied term

This is a term that the parties have not agreed should apply and instead will apply to the contract because of the common law, custom or an Act of Parliament.

A term is express where the parties have agreed on the term themselves and it is included in their contract. A term is implied where it is included in the contract not by the parties' own agreement but by implication. This occurs where an Act of Parliament, such as the Sale of Goods Act 1979, implies terms into a contract that stipulate that the goods sold must be of satisfactory quality (s.14(2)). The courts can imply a term in circumstances such as where such a term is required to give business efficacy to the contract. Terms can also be implied through custom and practice. In Chapter 4 we will look at how implied terms can be excluded from a contract.

On-the-spot question

 Snow Ltd has purchased a brand new lorry from Auto Lorry Ltd. The parties have verbally agreed that:

- the lorry is three years old;
- the lorry has only done 25,000 miles;
- the terms implied by the Sale of Goods Act 1979 do not apply to this contract.

How would you describe these terms?

Classification of terms

It is really important that you appreciate how terms are classified, as the classification of terms will be significant if a term is breached.

Conditions

A condition is a term that goes to the root of the contract. It is an important term of the contract and if breached it will allow the innocent party to repudiate the contract and/or claim damages. The parties can decide in a contract whether a particular term will be a condition by defining the term as such or by describing it as being of the essence. If the parties have not classified the term then the courts can determine whether the term will be treated as a condition or a warranty.

Warranties

A warranty is a less important term of the contract and if breached will entitle the innocent party to claim damages.

Innominate terms

Key definition: Innominate terms

This is a term that is not classified as either a condition or warranty and if the term is breached, only then will the courts determine whether the breach has deprived the innocent party of substantially the entire benefit of the contract. If it has deprived the innocent party of substantially the entire benefit of the contract, then the courts will classify this as a condition.

Traditionally, the courts have looked at the importance of the term in the contract before classifying it as either a condition or a warranty (see *Poussard v Spiers & Pond* (1876) 1 QBD 410). This has required the court to look at whether the term goes to the root of the contract. However, the Court of Appeal in *Hongkong Fir Shipping Co Ltd v Kawasaki Kisen Kaisha Ltd (The Hongkong Fir)* [1962] 2 QB 2 held that where a term was unclassified by the parties then the court could treat the term as innominate. The courts would look at the seriousness of the breach and not the initial importance of the term to the contract. If the breach were to deprive the innocent party of substantially the entire benefit of the contract then it would be classified as a condition.

DISCHARGE OF THE CONTRACT

A contract can be discharged in a number of ways. It is important that you understand how these occur.

Performance

First, the contract can be discharged by performance. This is where the parties have performed their contractual obligations as agreed.

Agreement

Second, the parties may choose to discharge the contract by agreement. This is the voluntary waiver of any outstanding obligations that have yet to be fulfilled. This might occur where Snow Ltd has contracted with Mrs Richards to build an extension, and subsequently, due to Mrs Richard's losing her job, they agree to discharge their obligations.

Frustration

Key definition: Frustration

A contract will be discharged where it is frustrated. At common law, frustration only discharges contracts where it is no longer possible to perform the contract due to impossibility, illegality or where the contract has become something that is radically different from what the parties have undertaken in the contract.

Third, a contract can be discharged by frustration. This is where the contractual obligations cannot be performed due to impossibility or illegality, or have become something that is radically different from what the parties have undertaken in the contract (see *Davis Contractors v Fareham Urban DC* [1956] AC 696). If the contract is held to have been frustrated, then the contract is treated as if it never occurred and the parties' obligations are discharged. Examples of what can amount to frustration include the destruction of the subject matter of the contract (*Taylor v Caldwell* (1863) 3 B & S 826) or the frustration of purpose, as this would render it impossible to perform your obligations. The outbreak of war is an example of illegality preventing a contract from being performed, as the contract if performed would involve trading with the enemy.

Where a party is seeking to discharge the contract on grounds of frustration it is important to note that the reason why the contract is frustrated must not be self-induced: that party must not be the cause of the frustrating event. The event must not have been foreseeable at the time of contract, as otherwise the parties would have been aware of the likelihood of it occurring.

Just because the contract has become more expensive to perform will not amount to frustration. The coronation cases illustrate when the cancellation of an event will, or will not, amount to frustration. King Edward VII was due to be crowned and before the coronation took place the king became very ill. This triggered the cancellation of the coronation and a subsequent naval review. In *Krell v Henry* [1903] 2 KB 740 a room had been rented in order to watch the coronation procession and it was successfully argued that the contract was frustrated due to the fact that purpose of the contract no longer existed. This was because both parties understood that the room was specifically hired in order to watch the coronation, rather than simply being a contract to hire a room. Following the coronation there was to have been a royal review of the British fleet. The Royal Navy had assembled off Herne Bay in Kent, and Hutton had contracted to hire a boat to view the ships. The royal review was cancelled and Hutton sought to argue that the contract was frustrated. In *Herne Bay Steam Boat Co v Hutton* [1903] 2 KB 683 the Court of Appeal held that the contract was not frustrated as the purpose of the contract was unaffected by the cancellation, as the contract was just for the hire of a boat and it was still possible for Hutton to hire the boat and visit the assembled fleet.

Prior to the enactment of the Law Reform (Frustrated Contracts) Act 1943 (LR(FC)A 1943), any money that had been paid in advance was not recoverable unless there had been a total failure of consideration (*Fibrosa Spolka Akcyjna v Fairbairn Lawson Combe Barbour Ltd* [1943] AC 32). If there had not been a total of failure of consideration, then the money was not recoverable. If there had been a total failure of consideration the party returning the money could not make a deduction to cover her own expenses. Section 1(2) of the LR(FC)A 1943 changes this position and permits all money paid prior to the frustrating event to be recovered and allows a deduction to be made to cover the other party's expenses. The Act also stated that any money due prior to the frustrating event was no longer payable.

Section 1(3) of the LR(FC)A 1943 permits the party who has provided a valuable benefit to the other party to recover a sum representing the benefit, which will be determined by the court.

On-the-spot question

? London has won the bid to host a big sporting competition that will take place next July. Amanda lives opposite the main venue and wishes to have a loft extension so that she can invite her friends and family to watch some of the events from her house. Based on the plans for the venue she should be able to have a good view of many of the sporting events. Amanda contacts Snow Ltd and arranges for a sales representative to visit her house. Amanda informs the sales representative that she wishes to have a loft extension built in time for next January. Work will commence in two months' time. Seven weeks later Amanda finds out that London will no longer be hosting the big sport competition and contacts Snow Ltd to inform them that based on her knowledge of contract law the contract is now frustrated.

Is Amanda correct? Has the contract been discharged due to frustration?

Breach

Figure 3.3 Effect of a breach of a condition

The final way that a contract may be discharged is where one of the parties has committed a repudiatory breach of the contract. Where a condition has been breached the innocent party may choose to treat the breach as amounting to a repudiatory breach and this will discharge the contract. The innocent party may still obtain damages from the defendant. Alternatively, the innocent party may affirm the breach and thus choose to keep the contract alive (see Figure 3.3). He may still obtain damages for the breach. Sometimes a party may inform the other party that there will not be breach of contract before the breach occurs. This is known as an anticipatory breach. The innocent party may be able to affirm the breach and continue with their own obligations and thus will be able to attempt to recover the full contractual amount owed (see *White & Carter (Councils) Ltd v McGregor* [1962] AC 413).

REMEDIES FOR BREACH OF CONTRACT

In Chapter 2 we saw how the courts can award both common law and equitable remedies. Where there is a breach of contract the innocent party, depending on how the term is classified, may have a right to repudiate the contract. The usual remedy for breach of contract is common law damages. The measure of damages is intended to protect the claimant's expectation interest, that is to seek to put the claimant in the financial position that she would have been in had the defendant performed his contractual obligations. However, the claimant could instead seek to recover her reliance interest, which would recover any expenses incurred in performing her obligations. The courts may refuse to permit the claimant to recover her expectation interest where it is impossible to say with certainty just what the claimant's financial position would have been had the contract been performed. Where this occurs the courts may calculate damages according to the reliance interest (see *Anglia Television Ltd v Reed* [1972] 1 QB 60).

The claimant must prove that the defendant caused her losses and that the damages sought cannot be too remote and must be foreseeable (see *Hadley v Baxendale* (1854) 9 Ex 341). The claimant would also be expected to take reasonable steps to mitigate her losses, such as by attempting to find an alternative supplier or contractor to undertake the work.

A number of equitable remedies are available such as injunctions and specific performance. We will explore injunctions in Chapter 5 and by awarding an injunction the courts are preventing a party from breaching their obligations. Specific performance is a remedy that is rarely awarded as it compels performance of a contractual obligation and the courts prefer to award damages where there has been a breach.

SUMMARY

- In order to have a contract there must be an offer that has been accepted, there must be consideration, the parties must have intended to create legal relations and also have the capacity to contract.
- A contract may be set aside for a number of reasons including misrepresentation and mistake.
- The contract will be discharged where there has been performance, agreement, breach or frustration.

- Where a term of the contract has been breached, the remedy that is available will depend on the classification of the term.

FURTHER READING

Beatson, J., Burrows, A. and Cartwright, J. *Anson's Law of Contract*, 29th edn (Oxford University Press, 2010) – this is an authoritative text on contract law and provides academic commentary on the key areas covered in this chapter.

McKendrick, E. *Contract Law*, 10th edn (Palgrave, 2013) – refer to this text for an accessible and clear introduction to the key areas of contract law.

Monaghan, C. and Monaghan, N. *Beginning Contract Law* (Routledge, 2013) – this is an introductory text and explores the key areas covered in this chapter in a succinct manner.

Stone, R. *The Modern Law of Contract*, 10th edn (Routledge, 2013) – this text provides additional coverage of the material in this chapter.

Chapter 4
Contracts for the sale of goods

LEARNING OBJECTIVES

After reading this chapter, you should be able to:

- appreciate what is meant by a contract for the sale of goods;
- understand the effect of the Sale of Goods Act 1979;
- comprehend the reason for including certain clauses in a contract; and
- demonstrate an awareness of the international dimensions of contract law.

INTRODUCTION

In Chapter 3 we explored the law of contract and considered how a contract is formed, the remedies for breaching the contract and how it is discharged. In this chapter we will look at how contracts are used by businesses and the purpose served by each of the clauses in the contract (see Figure 4.1). We will focus on a contract for the sale of goods and this will enable us to consider the key clauses in a commercial contract and the Sale of Goods Act 1979 (SGA 1979). The law that we shall consider in this chapter will be as applicable to a small high street grocery chain, as it will be to a leading supermarket.

WHAT IS A CONTRACT FOR THE SALE OF GOODS?

In this chapter we will look at the various issues encountered by Kings Abbots Engineering Ltd (KAE), which is a small business based in England that manufactures a range of grinding machines for use in the motor industry. If KAE entered into a contract to sell 1,000 grinding machines to Guildhall Motors Ltd (GML), then so long as the statutory requirements are met under s.2(1) SGA 1979, this would be a contract for the sale of goods. These requirements must be met regardless of whether the contract is made in writing, orally or implied by the parties' conduct (s.4 SGA 1979).

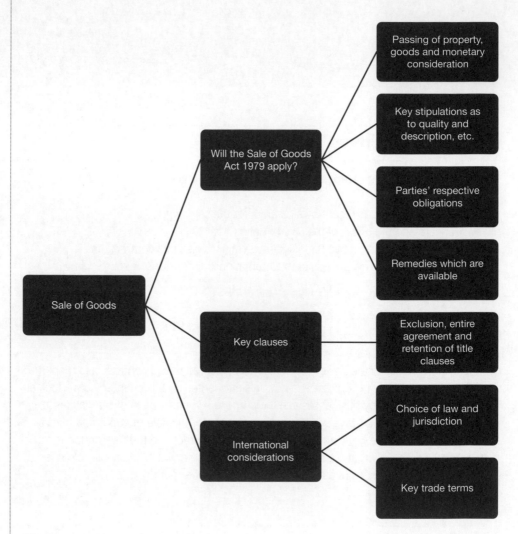

Figure 4.1 Chapter overview

Key definition: Contract for the sale of goods

According to s.2(1) SGA 1979, 'A contract of sale of goods is a contract by which the seller transfers or agrees to transfer the property in goods to the buyer for a money consideration, called the price.'

Looking at the definition above the first requirement that must be satisfied is that the grinding machines are goods. It is necessary to consider the statutory definition of goods under s.61(1), which states that goods include such things as 'all personal chattels'. The grinding machine would be a personal chattel. Interestingly, your pet dog and hamster would also fall under the statutory definition of goods, as would crops grown by a farmer. The second requirement is that KAE, as the seller in the contract with GML, must transfer or will agree to transfer the property in the goods. Here, property does not mean the physical delivery of the grinding machines, rather, it means something more than the mere physical goods, as it relates to the legal title to the goods, i.e. ownership. Finally, the third requirement that needs to be satisfied is that there must be monetary consideration. This is the significant difference to other types of contracts where consideration can be non-monetary, such as where the parties barter, i.e. exchange goods.

Points to consider about s.2(1) SGA 1979

1 Monetary consideration

A contract where the parties exchange goods via bartering is not a contract for the sale of goods. Where the parties are exchanging goods but one party agrees to pay a sum to make up the lower value of the goods that he is exchanging, then this contract could fall within the s.2(1) definition. An example of this is the case of *Aldridge v Johnson* (1857) 119 ER 1476.

2 Goods?

However, it is often difficult to determine whether the SGA 1979 applies to certain types of contracts. A contemporary issue is computer software. In *St Albans City and DC v International Computers Ltd* [1996] 4 All ER 481, the Court of Appeal considered whether computer software was a good for the purposes of the SGA 1979. In his judgment Glidewell LJ observed that:

- if a disc that contains computer software is sold or hired then it would constitute a good for the purposes of the SGA 1979 and the Supply of Goods and Services Act 1982. His Lordship drew an analogy with an instruction manual or a videotape which contained these instructions;
- if the content of the disc was merely installed onto the computer by the company supplying the software and was then taken away it would not be a good;
- the program (software) was held not to be a good within the statutory definition.

3 Passing of property

In *London Borough of Southwark v IBM UK Ltd* [2011] EWHC 549 (TCC) it was held that as the software had been supplied under a licence there had not been a transfer of property as required by s.2(1) SGA 1979. This meant that the court did not have to consider whether the software was a good.

Future goods

It is important to note that had KAE entered into the contract of sale with GML and it had not yet manufactured the grinding machines, then the goods would be classified as future goods. It would still be a valid contract, known as an agreement to sell, notwithstanding the fact that the goods do not exist at the time when the contract was entered into (s.5 SGA 1979).

SALE OF GOODS ACT 1979

The SGA 1979 applies to both business-to-business contracts, business-to-consumer contracts, and finally to consumer-to-consumer contracts. In this chapter we will focus on business-to-business contracts. However, it should be noted that different rules can apply to each of the above contracts and so you must be careful to distinguish which type of contract you are dealing with.

The SGA 1979 contains rules that govern a number of important aspects of the contract. These include:

- stipulations relating to the time of payment, the requirement that the seller has a right to transfer the legal title, the quality and description of the goods;
- where the goods have perished before, or after, the contract has been entered into;
- the transfer of the property in the goods;
- the passing of the risk in the goods;
- the ability of the seller to transfer the physical goods to the buyer, while retaining the title (property) in the goods;
- the rule that the seller cannot transfer good title if he does not have this himself;
- the remedies available to both the buyer and the seller in the event that the contract has been breached;
- the rules relating to the delivery, acceptance and inspection of the goods.

We shall consider each of these in turn and as we do this we will look at some of the common clauses that you will find in a commercial contract. These are known as boilerplate clauses as they are common clauses that you would expect to see in a contract of this type. This will enable you to see how these clauses relate to the legal rules.

SALE OF GOODS DISTINGUISHED FROM A CONTRACT FOR THE SUPPLY OF GOODS AND SERVICES

Where you are contracting to obtain services and the goods will be supplied as incidental to this contract, in that case the contract will not be for the sale of goods, rather it will be a contract for the supply of goods and services and will be governed by the Supply of Goods and Services Act 1982. Examples of this type of contract include a builder who builds a new kitchen and as part of the contract price includes all appliances and white goods.

KEY ISSUES

However, before we proceed there are a number of key issues to consider.

Does English and Welsh law apply?

The first issue to consider is what the choice of law and the choice of jurisdiction will be.

Key definition: Choice of law

This means which country's law will govern the contract. It is important as every country will have its own law and the parties may not be familiar with another country's law. Where the parties are based within the European Union, the Rome II Regulation will regulate which country's law will apply.

Key definition: Choice of jurisdiction

This means which country's courts will resolve the dispute. Where the parties are based within the European Union, the Brussels I Regulation will regulate which country's courts will have jurisdiction.

The parties, subject to any rules to the contrary, will be able to determine which country's law will govern the contract. As KAE is a company based in England it will be familiar with the law of England and Wales and therefore would prefer to have the contract governed by this law. However, GML could be based in Scotland and thus it could prefer to have the contract governed by the law of Scotland. The parties would need to negotiate as to which law will govern the contract. Even if Scottish law were to govern the contract, then most of the SGA 1979 would still apply. However, if GML wished to use French law to govern the contract, then French law would apply, rather than the SGA 1979. A choice of jurisdiction clause stipulates which country's courts will resolve any dispute between the parties in the event that there has been an alleged breach of contract.

Key concepts in agreeing which clauses apply

Key definition: Standard form contract

This type of contract contains the key terms and would be offered by a seller to all buyers of its products. The buyer would then contract on the seller's terms without negotiating the terms on an individual basis.

Key definition: Battle of the forms

This is where both parties are determined to contract on their own standard form contracts and try to make the other party accept their terms.

The parties' bargaining positions will be important here. The party in the strongest bargaining position will be able to determine whether the contract is pro-buyer or pro-seller. While the parties do have freedom of contract and could agree any price they wished for the goods, the common law and statute will regulate the validity of certain clauses. It is common for the parties to contract using standard form contracts and such a contract will be supplied by the party on whose terms the contract will be entered into. Parties will often seek to contract on their own terms and they will attempt to force the other side to signify acceptance of their terms. This is known as the battle of the forms and an example of this is *Butler Machine Tool Co v Ex-cell-o Corp (England)* [1979] 1 WLR 401.

Key obligations and the importance of certainty

The contract should state the parties' respective obligations. KAE's contract with GML would contain the following obligations:

- KAE will sell 1,000 grinding machines to GML;
- KAE will deliver the 1,000 grinding machines to GML's premise on 5 August 2016;
- GML will purchase the 1,000 grinding machines and agrees to pay £52 per item;

- GML will pay KAE the entire contract price no later than 30 working days after the 1,000 grinding machines have been delivered to GML's premises.

Clearly, these are not all the obligations but you will notice that we have encountered a problem: KAE makes a number of different grinding machines and GML has six factories across the United Kingdom. To avoid the contract being void for uncertainty the parties would include a clause in their contract that would define the key terms. This interpretative provision would ensure that the validity of the contract could not be challenged by a party seeking to have the contract invalidated (see *G Scammell Nephew Ltd v HC &JG Ouston* [1941] AC 251). In *Baird Textile Holdings Ltd v Marks & Spencer plc* [2001] EWCA Civ 274 the Court of Appeal held that a contract was void because there was no certainty as to the quantity of goods to be purchased or the price to be paid for the goods.

But what would happen if the parties neglected to include a fixed price? This would not affect the validity of contract so long as the parties had included a mechanism for determining the price of the goods or it could be determined by their course of dealing (s.8(1) SGA 1979). An example of this would be a contract to supply barrels of oil over a ten-year period. As the price of oil fluctuates the parties would not set a fixed price, but would instead include a method of calculating the monthly price payable at the date of payment. The method of calculation must be objectively verifiable. If none of these were present in the contract then as a general rule the contract would be void for uncertainty (see *May and Butcher Ltd v The King* [1934] 2 KB 17). However, s.8(2) SGA 1979 states that in the absence of a determinable price the buyer must pay a reasonable price.

On-the-spot question

? KAE and GML's contract states that the choice of law and choice of jurisdiction will be the United Kingdom. The price of the grinding machine is omitted and instead the parties have inserted a clause that states that 'the price of each unit will be determined by the parties at a future date'. GML agrees to purchase a number of grinding machines on a monthly basis, over a period of time to be determined at a later date.

Advise KAE as to whether there are any problems with the above contract.

KEY PROVISIONS OF THE SALE OF GOODS ACT 1979

We will now consider the key provisions of the Sale of Goods Act 1979.

Stipulations relating to the time of payment, legal title, the quality and description of the goods.

Stipulations about time

The time of payment is not treated as being 'of the essence of a contract of sale' (s.10(1) SGA 1979). This means that if the buyer does not pay on the agreed date then the seller will be unable to claim that there has been a repudiatory breach of the contract.

Key definition: Of the essence

You will remember from Chapter 3 that there is a distinction between conditions and warranties. The phrase 'of the essence' means that the term is to be treated as a condition and will permit the innocent party to discharge the contract.

However, the parties are permitted to expressly state that time of payment is of the essence. Other stipulations as to time will depend on the term of the contract (s.8(2)). In *Hartley v Hymans* [1920] 3 KB 475 it was held that time of delivery is of the essence.

Stipulation as to title

It is important that KAE has the right to sell the goods to GML. Section 12(1) states that there is an implied condition that the seller must have the right to sell the goods and this means that the seller must have title to the goods (or permission to sell on behalf of the title holder). In other words the seller must actually own the goods or be selling on behalf of another person. As we discussed above, it is possible to contract to sell goods that you do not yet own, but that you intend to acquire or manufacture in the future. Section 12(1) is a condition and if it is breached the buyer can repudiate the contract. In the case of *Rowland v Divall* [1923] 2 KB 500 the Court of Appeal held that the buyer of a car that had turned out to be stolen could sue the seller and reclaim his purchase price, notwithstanding the fact that he no longer had the car and could not return it to the seller.

It is interesting to consider the effect of breaching s.12 (1), which is demonstrated in the Court of Appeal's decision in *Rowland v Divall* [1923] 2 KB 500.

KEY CASE ANALYSIS: *Rowland v Divall* **[1923] 2 K.B. 500**

Background

The claimant had purchased a car from the defendant. He had used the car for a number of months. However, it transpired that the car did not belong to the defendant and the claimant was forced to return the car to its legal owner.

Principle established

The claimant was able to recover the purchase price, despite being unable to return the car to the defendant. This was because there had been a total failure of consideration as the claimant had contract to purchase the legal title to the car and had paid the purchase price in return for this. As the defendant could not transfer legal title to him there had been no consideration.

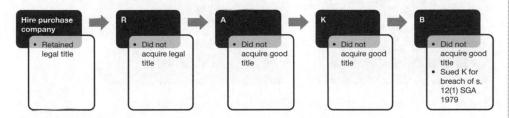

Figure 4.2 *Butterworth v Kingsway Motors Ltd* [1954] 1 WLR 1286

A similar decision was reached in *Butterworth v Kingsway Motors Ltd* [1954] 1 WLR 1286 where a car was supplied on hire-credit to R who had then sold the car to A, despite the fact that the hire-purchase company had legal title. Eventually, the car was purchased by K (the defendant), who believed that it had acquired legal title. K subsequently sold the car to B (the claimant). B found out that the car was still owned by the hire purchase company and successfully repudiated the contract and demanded the return of the full purchase price. Controversially, as there had been a total failure of consideration, B was entitled to a full refund from K despite having used the car for nearly a year (see Figure 4.2).

Section 12(2)(a) and (b) are implied warranties and state that the goods are free from any encumbrances and that the buyer will enjoy quiet possession of the goods. The implied warranty that the buyer will enjoy quiet possession extends beyond the date of contract and therefore if the seller had a right to sell the goods when the parties contracted, but if at a later date something occurred that meant that the buyer would no longer have quiet enjoyment of the goods, then in this example there would not be a breach of s.12(1). However, there would be a breach of s.12(2)(b). This occurred in the case of *Microbeads AF v Vinhurst Road Markings* [1975] 1 WLR 218 where road marking machines were sold to the buyer and it later turned out that a third party had subsequently acquired the patent to a similar machine.

Stipulation as to description

Figure 4.3 Distinction between specific and unascertained goods

---

Key definition: Specific goods

A definition is provided by s.61(1) SGA 1979, which states '"specific goods" means goods identified and agreed on at the time a contract of sale is made and includes an undivided share, specified as a fraction or percentage, of goods identified and agreed on as aforesaid'.

Key definition: Unascertained goods

No definition is provided by the SGA 1979. Unascertained goods are those goods that are not identifiable or agreed upon at the time of contract. An example of this would be a contract to purchase 100,000 cans of tinned fruit. The manufacturer would be able to supply any 100,000 cans that correspond to the contractual description.

According to s.13(1) SGA 1979 there is an implied condition in every contract that where goods have been sold by description then the goods supplied must correspond with that description. This requirement applies to both unascertained goods and specific goods and covers goods that you have purchased prior to seeing them such as via mail order and also to goods that you have viewed prior to the purchase (see Figure 4.3). In *Grant v Australian Knitting Mills Ltd* [1936] AC 85, the Privy Council held that s.13 applied to goods purchased from a shop counter. Under the perfect tender rule, the courts have permitted the buyer to reject the goods where there is any inconsistency between the description and the actual goods. An example of this is *FW Moore & Co Ltd v Landauer & Co* [1921] 2 KB 519 where cans of tinned fruit were described as being in cases of 30 tins. Half the cases supplied only contained 24 tins. Despite there being no difference in the market value of the goods supplied, the buyer was entitled to reject all the goods supplied. Clearly, this is a harsh rule as the buyer was not disadvantaged and used s.13 to escape contract. The courts have limited the protection afforded by s.13 by asking whether the words used to describe the goods had become an essential term of the contract. In *Harlingdon and Leinster Enterprises Ltd v Christopher Hull Fine Art Ltd* [1991] 1 QB 564 the Court of Appeal held that there could not be a sale by description where the parties had not intended that the buyer would rely upon a description of a painting as being by Gabriele Münter.

Stipulation as to quality

There is an implied condition under s.14(2) that the goods supplied will be of satisfactory quality. The goods must be suitable for their common purpose and the courts will take into account a number of factors include age, price and safety to determine whether there had been a breach of s.14(2). Section 14(2) will not give rise to liability where the goods are suitable for a common purpose but are not suitable to the buyer's undisclosed particular purpose (see *Griffiths v Peter Conway Ltd* [1939] 1 All ER 685).

Stipulation as fitness for particular purpose

Section 14(3) states that where the buyer has expressly or impliedly made known to the seller the particular purpose for which she requires the goods, then the goods supplied must be suitable for that particular purpose (see *Priest v Last* [1903] 2 KB 148). It must be reasonable for the buyer to rely on the seller's skill and expertise. Section 14(3) is an implied condition.

KEY CASE ANALYSIS: *Teheran-Europe Co Ltd v ST Belton (Tractors) Ltd (No 1)* **[1968] 2 QB 545**

Background

The seller did not know that the compressors supplied under the contract to the buyer were actually going to be used in Iran. An agent acting on behalf of the undisclosed principal had purchased the goods. The compressors were not suitable for use in Iran and the sellers were sued for breach of s.14(3).

Principle established

The Court of Appeal held that there was no breach of s.14(3) because the buyer had not relied upon the seller's skill and judgment. This was because the buyer was purchasing goods for its home market and the court said that buyer would know more about this market than the seller possibly could.

Stipulation that the goods must conform to the sample

Section 15 is an implied condition and states that where goods are sold by sample the goods must correspond with the quality of the sample.

Restrictions on ss.13–15

It is important to note that s.15A SGA 1979 restricts the buyer from treating a minor breach of ss.13–15 that is so slight as a breach of a condition. Instead the breach is treated as a breach of a warranty.

Exclusion clauses

The parties can agree to include a clause in the contract that will exclude the terms implied under ss.13–15 (s.55 SGA 1979). This clause is known as an exclusion clause and is regulated by the Unfair Contract Terms Act 1977 (UCTA 1977). An exclusion clause must be incorporated into the contract, must cover the breach and be valid under UCTA 1977. The clause can be incorporated by being included into the contract, by being brought to the notice of the other party at the time of contract or by a course of dealing. In *Olley v Marlborough Court Ltd* [1949] 1 KB 532, an exclusion clause was not incorporated as it had only been brought to the other party's attention after the contract had been entered into. That particular clause had sought to exclude liability for damage or loss to guests' belongings. The notice should have been at the check-in desk where the contract was concluded and not just in the hotel bedroom. The clause must cover the breach and if it does not then the defendant will be liable. A rule known as the *contra proferentem* rule construes ambiguous clauses in favour of the party that the clause is being used against. Finally, liability for breach of s.12 SGA 1979 cannot be excluded (s.6(1) UCTA 1977) and ss.13–15 SGA 1979 cannot be excluded where the buyer is a consumer (s.6(2) UCTA 1977). Sections 13–15 can only be excluded where the buyer is a business and then only if it is reasonable to have included the exclusion clause (s.6(3) UCTA 1977). Reasonableness is determined with reference to s.11 and schedule 2 of UCTA 1977. Where the parties are businesses of equal bargaining power, there is a presumption that the clause will be reasonable (see *Watford Electronics Ltd v Sanderson CFL Ltd* [2001] EWCA Civ 317).

Replacing the implied conditions with express warranties

Key definition: Implied terms

A term implied into a contract by custom and practice, the common law and by statute.

Key definition: Express terms

A term that the parties have expressly agreed. There can be express terms in both a written and an oral contract.

Key definition: Conditions

An important term of the contract that if breached will permit the innocent party to repudiate the contract (i.e. bring it to an end) and/or claim damages.

Key definition: Warranties

A less important term of the contract that if breached will only permit the innocent party to claim damages.

The parties could agree in a business-to-business contract to replace the implied terms with express warranties. These could replicate the protection offered by the SGA 1979 without permitting the buyer to reject the goods. Instead the contract could agree a range of remedies.

Where the goods have perished before or after the contract has been entered into

Imagine that KAE has contracted to sell a lorry (registration number 134567 YBN) to Fred's Second Hand Motors. Unbeknown to the parties, the lorry had perished in a fire two hours before the contract was entered into. If this were to occur the contract would be void, as s.6 SGA 1979 states that where the goods are specific goods, which the lorry clearly is as it has an identifiable registration number and could not be substituted, the contract would be void. The consequence of the contract being void is that the obligations to pay and deliver the goods no longer exist. If the goods were unascertained goods (i.e. 1,000 grinding machines) we would have to look at common law frustration to see whether the contract could be discharged.

The transfer of property in the goods

As we have discussed above, property refers to legal title. The SGA 1979 established rules about the passing of property from the seller to the buyer. This is important because if KAE agreed to sell 1,000 grinding machines to GML on 1 May and payment was due on 1 June, with delivery taking place on 16 June, what would happen if KAE became insolvent on 12 June? Could GML argue the grinding machines belonged to it or would GML only be an unsecured creditor and could only recover (if possible) its purchase price? To answer these questions we must consider the SGA 1979 and distinguish between specific and unascertained goods:

1   As the grinding machines are manufactured goods and KAE has a choice as to which of the thousands it produces to attach to the contract and deliver on 16 June, the goods would be classified as unascertained goods, as until delivery took place there was no unconditional appropriation of the goods to the contract (see *Carlos Federspiel & Co SA v Charles Twigg & Co Ltd* [1957] 1 Lloyd's Rep 240).
2   Section 16 SGA 1979 states that property in unascertained goods cannot pass until the goods have become ascertained. Here, the passing of property would occur on delivery.
3   If the contract was silent as to when property would pass then we would refer to s.18 and the five rules that deal with this. Rule 5 states that property in unascertained goods passes when they become unconditionally appropriated to the contract.
4   This means that in the above scenario the property in the goods would remain with KAE and GML would only have a right to recover its purchase price as an unsecured creditor.

Had the goods been specific goods (i.e. a famous painting) then property in the goods can pass at any time as it is clear which particular good is attached to the contract (s.17 SGA

1979). Where the contract is silent as to the passing of property in specific goods, s.18 Rule 1 states that property passes at the time the contract is made. This is regardless of whether payment has been made or the goods have been delivered.

On-the-spot question

? Lucy manufactures handmade ceramic plates and contracts to sell 100 blue plates to Stuart on 1 June in return for an upfront payment of £1,300. The parties agree that the property in the goods will pass at the time of contract. As Stuart is away on holiday he agrees to collect the goods in two weeks' time on 14 June. Between 3 and 9 June Lucy makes 300 blue plates and places 100 of the plates in a box marked 'Stuart'. Lucy seals the box and places it in her shed. On 13 June Lucy is declared bankrupt.

Advise Stuart as to whether he owns the 100 blue plates.

The passing of risk in the goods

If a party has the risk in the goods then they will be responsible if the goods are damaged or stolen. If it is the seller then he will be in breach of contract if he cannot supply the goods; alternatively, if it is the buyer who has the risk in the goods and has not yet paid the contract price and the goods are damaged she must pay for the goods. Section 20(1) SGA 1979 states that the risk in the goods passes with property. It is possible to expressly state in the contract when risk will pass.

The ability of the seller to transfer the physical goods to the buyer, while retaining the title (property) in the goods

---

Key definition: Retention of title clause

The seller will be permitted to retain title to the goods while transferring the physical goods to the buyer. Title will pass to the buyer once he has paid the full purchase price to the seller.

Section 19 SGA 1979 permits the seller to retain the right of disposal in the goods. This allows the seller to retain the title (property) in the goods until certain conditions such as payment have been met. If a retention of title clause is included in the contract the seller will retain title to the goods and can deliver the goods to the buyer to sell and use in its manufacturing processes (*Aluminium Industrie Vaassen BV v Romalpa Aluminium* [1976] 1 WLR 676). The buyer will not own the goods but is able to sell the goods to third parties who will acquire good title (see s.25 SGA 1979). The buyer can also use the goods in her manufacturing process. If this occurs and the goods are irretrievably incorporated into another product then the seller will no longer have title (see *Re Peachdart Ltd* [1984] Ch 131). The courts have been reluctant to permit sellers to use increasingly elaborate retention of title clauses and this is an area of law that requires careful consideration.

The rule that the seller cannot transfer good title if he does not have good title

The *nemo dat* rule states that the seller can transfer good title to the buyer if he himself does not have good title to the goods. This principle exists to protect the original owner of the goods who can demand the goods back from the innocent buyer. Failure to return the goods will give rise to liability under the tort of conversion (see Torts (Interference with Goods) Act 1977). Section 21 SGA 1979 reiterates the *nemo dat* rule. There are a number of exceptions to the *nemo dat* rule and three of these are included in the Act (see ss.23–25). The *nemo dat* rule is regarded as harsh to the innocent purchaser who is unaware that the goods that they are buying belong to someone other than the seller.

The remedies available to both the buyer and the seller

The buyer's remedies for breach of contract are contained in ss.51–53 SGA 1979. The power under s.52 to ask the court for specific performance is restrictive and is only available against specific or ascertained goods (*Re Wait* [1927] 1 Ch 606). The seller has personal remedies against the buyer for breach of contract under ss.49–50 and remedies against the goods. For example, if the seller is unpaid she can exercise a lien over the goods (s.41).

Delivery, acceptance and inspection of the goods

The SGA 1979 contains rules about how the contract is to be performed. In the absence of an indication to the contrary, the place of delivery is the seller's premises (s.29). When the goods are delivered the buyer has a right to inspect the goods (s.34). Section 35 concerns the rules relating to the acceptance of the goods. If the buyer accepts the goods then she cannot reject these upon discovering a fault at a later date.

KEY CLAUSES

We shall now look at a number of important clauses that you would expect to find in a contract for the sale of goods.

Force majeure clauses

A *force majeure* clause is intended to provide more protection than only relying on frustration to discharge the contract. The parties can list a number of occurrences that will amount to a *force majeure* event. This is wider than the narrow approach of frustration that only applies if it is impossible, illegal to perform the contract, or if the frustrating event has caused the contract to become something radically different from the one entered into (see *Davis Contractors v Fareham Urban DC* [1956] AC 696). No party will be liable for non-performance caused as a result of one of these events occurring. Unlike frustration, which will discharge the contract, a *force majeure* event could allow for the contract to be suspended until it is possible to complete the contractual obligations.

Entire agreement clause and non-reliance clause

At common law the parol evidence rule excludes any other alleged terms from the contract where the contract is written. This ensures certainty. However, there are a number of exceptions at common law, such as where the contract is partly oral and where there is a collateral contract existing alongside the main contract. To protect the parties it is common to include an entire agreement clause that states that the written contract is the entire agreement between the parties. It is common to also include a non-reliance clause that seeks to prevent a party from claiming that they relied upon any representations when entering into the contract.

Third party rights and non-assignment

As we have seen in Chapter 3, the Contract (Rights of Third Parties) Act 1999 has created a statutory exception to the common law doctrine of privity of contract. Many contracts include a clause excluding any possible third party rights from being created. The parties may wish to exclude the possibility of one party assigning its contractual obligations to a third party.

Alternative Dispute Resolution

The parties may wish to include an Alternative Dispute Resolution (ADR) clause in their contract. ADR is a means to resolving the dispute without going to court. There are a number of different types of ADR such as mediation, negotiation, expert determination and arbitration. Each of these different types has advantages and disadvantages.

INTERNATIONAL SALES CONTRACTS

In practice your business will want to conduct trade with companies based in different jurisdictions. This is because we live in an increasingly globalised world. KAE may wish to sell its grinding machines to a buyer based in the United States or South Korea. As we saw above when we looked at which country's law would govern the contract and which court would have jurisdiction to hear a dispute, it can be difficult to find a law that both parties can agree upon. English law and its courts have an excellent international reputation and many parties based outside this jurisdiction choose to contract using English law.

Vienna Convention on Contracts for the International Sale of Goods

In an international sales contract between KAE and a seller based overseas there is a neutral sales law that could be used as this is known as the Vienna Convention on Contracts for the International Sale of Goods (CISG). CISG is not comprehensive and you would need to choose a law to govern the contract where CISG does not provide an answer.

Trade terms

If KAE were to contract to sell 10,000 grinding machines to a seller based in Mexico and the contract will be governed by English law, then the parties must ensure that they agree upon *inter alia* who will deliver the goods to the port of shipment, pay the loading costs, arrange space in the container ship, contract with the ship's owners for carriage and insure the goods. At common law there are a number of trade terms that can be used as shorthand to assign the parties' responsibilities. For example, the trade term f.o.b. in its classic meaning, obliges the seller to deliver the goods to the port of shipment and pay the loading costs. Beyond this, all other responsibilities are with the buyer. The International Chamber of Commerce has developed its own trade terms known as INCOTERMS that are different to those developed by the common law.

SUMMARY

- The Sale of Goods Act 1979 will imply a number of important stipulations as to title, quality and description into a contract for the sale of goods.
- A contract will contain a number of important clauses that are required to give effect to the parties' intentions and to prevent future dispute and liability.
- A contract for the sale of goods will often have an international dimension and it is important to consider the additional issues that will arise.

FURTHER READING

Adams, J. and MacQueen, H. *Atiyah's Sale of Goods*, 12th edn (Pearson, 2010) – refer to this book for a detailed coverage of domestic sales law and an overview of CISG and trade terms.

Bridge, M. (ed.) *Benjamin's Sale of Goods*, 8th edn (Sweet & Maxwell, 2010) – this is the authoritative guide to the Sale of Goods Act 1979.

Dobson, P. and Stokes, R. *Commercial Law*, 8th edn (Sweet & Maxwell, 2012) – this is an accessible textbook and provides a clear approach to the SGA 1979.

Goode, R. and McKendrick, E. *Goode on Commercial Law*, 4th edn (Penguin, 2010) – refer to this for an authoritative guide to domestic and international sales law.

Sealy, L. S. and Hooley, R. S. A. *Commercial Law: Text, Cases, and Materials*, 4th edn (Oxford University Press, 2008) – this is a useful addition to the above texts with extracts of relevant cases and academic opinion.

Chapter 5
Tort law

LEARNING OBJECTIVES

After reading this chapter, you should be able to:

- understand the distinction between the obligations imposed by contract law and tort law;
- appreciate how the law of torts affects businesses and how a business can be vicariously liable for the acts or omissions of its employees;
- comprehend how liability will arise in the tort of negligence and which types of loss will generally not be recoverable;
- understand how different torts protect a business's property, its reputation and the contracts that it enters into.

INTRODUCTION

In this chapter we will consider the impact of tort law or the law of torts on a business (Figure 5.1). A tort is a civil wrong and the common law and statute impose duties on individuals and businesses to avoid breaching a duty owed to another. Tort law is important as a business will be vicariously liable for the acts and omissions of its employees and will need to be aware that an employee who drives the company's lorry negligently, or who posts offensive comments about a rival business on his employer's website could result in the business being liable.

How is tort law different from contract law?

The difference between tort law and contract law is that in tort legal obligations arise irrespective of whether there is a contract between the claimant and defendant. This means that in contract law the parties will voluntarily contract and accept their obligations, whereas in tort the law imposes obligations that will be owed to others regardless of whether they have consented to them. That is not to say that the parties to a contract will have complete freedom to determine the extent of their obligations, as the law has restricted the freedom of contract by introducing rules on the validity of certain terms and by introducing mandatory obligations for particular types of contracts. The law of tort has

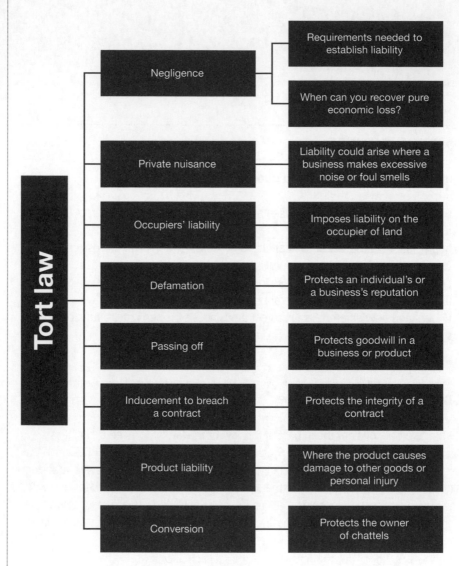

Figure 5.1 Key torts covered in this chapter

developed to establish that a duty of care will be owed in different circumstances and
seeks to regulate our conduct by imposing an obligation to avoid causing others loss. You
will see how the different torts arise and how a business will need to understand first its
legal obligations and thus try to avoid liability, and second the protection that is afforded to
it by tort law.

In this chapter we will consider how the material covered will relate to a fictional business,
Temple, Strand & Holborn Ltd (TSH Ltd). TSH Ltd specialises in fitting out shops.

Remedies

Unlike contract law the aim of damages in tort law is to put the claimant back in the position she was in prior to the tort occurring. Damages are intended to be compensatory in nature. There are different types of damages available, depending on the circumstances of the claim. In addition to damages a claimant may seek the court to award an equitable remedy such as an injunction. Injunctions are awarded at the court's discretion and are commonly sought in order to prevent a party from acting in a way that would amount to a civil wrong. For example, we will see below that the defendant could be liable where he passes off his goods as being associated with the claimants. An injunction could be awarded to prevent the defendant from selling these goods.

Temporary pre-trial injunctions

A party can apply for an interlocutory injunction that is a temporary restraint to prevent another party from acting in a certain way until the trial. The test for whether such an injunction should be awarded by the court was established in *American Cyanamid Co v Ethicon Ltd (No 1)* [1975] AC 396. In determining whether to award an interlocutory injunction, the court should take into account whether damages would be adequate compensation if the defendant were able to continue with the conduct that the claimant had objected to. A breach of an injunction amounts to contempt of court and the defendant could face a custodial sentence.

Burden of proof

It is important to note that the burden of proof is on the claimant and this requires the claimant to establish that on the balance of probabilities the defendant caused her loss. This standard is much lower than that which applies in criminal law, where the prosecution must establish that the defendant is guilty beyond reasonable doubt.

Limitation Act 1980

The claimant's ability to bring a claim in tort and contract is limited by the Limitation Act 1980. The claimant has six years from the date on which the tort occurred in order to bring a claim (s.2). However, for personal injury, or death, or for damage caused by defective products the time limit is three years (ss.11 and 11A). However, you should note that where there is a latent defect, which is where the claimant does not know that the defendant has been negligent, then the time limit will be three years from where the claimant had knowledge that there was a defect (s.14A). Section 14A does not apply where the defect causes personal injury. Section 14B imposes an overriding time limit of fifteen years.

Defences

There are a number of defences that the defendant can rely upon. These include where the claimant has consented to the risk, was committing an illegal act or was contributorily negligent. Examples of contributory negligence include where the defendant's negligent driving injured the claimant, but at the time of the accident the claimant was not wearing his seatbelt. In *Froom v Butcher* [1976] QB 286 the Court of Appeal held that as the injuries suffered would have been reduced or would not have occurred had a seatbelt be worn, the damages awarded should be reduced to reflect this. In *Froom* the damages were reduced by 20 per cent.

NEGLIGENCE

We will now look at the tort of negligence and explore the elements that must be established in order for the defendant to be liable.

The tort of negligence requires a number of elements to be established in order for the defendant to be liable. First, there must be a duty of care owed by the defendant to the claimant, which the defendant has breached. Second, the defendant's breach of that duty of care must cause the claimant's loss. This is the causation requirement. Finally, the loss, which the claimant is attempting to recover, must not be too remote.

Establishing a duty of care

The key case that established a general duty of care was *Donoghue v Stevenson* [1932] AC 562.

KEY CASE ANALYSIS: *Donoghue v Stevenson* [1932] AC 562

Background

The claimant's friend bought her an opaque bottle of ginger beer from a shop. She drank most of the ginger beer and found a decomposed snail at the bottom. The claimant was shocked and suffered gastroenteritis.

Principle established

The case established a general duty of care for negligence and enabled a consumer to sue the manufacturer when the product supplied through a third party was defective. This avoids the problem of the consumer not being able to sue the manufacturer in contract as there is no privity of contract between them. The House of Lords held that everyone owed a duty of care to your neighbour. This meant that the defendant must take reasonable steps to avoid an act or omission (a failure to act) that the defendant could reasonably foresee would be likely to injure the claimant. Lord Atkin stated:

> The rule that you are to love your neighbour becomes in law, you must not injure your neighbour; and the lawyer's question, Who is my neighbour? receives a restricted reply. You must take reasonable care to avoid acts or omissions which you can reasonably foresee would be likely to injure your neighbour. Who, then, in law is my neighbour? The answer seems to be – persons who are so closely and directly affected by my act that I ought reasonably to have them in contemplation as being so affected when I am directing my mind to the acts or omissions which are called in question. (at p. 580)

Donoghue v Stevenson was a landmark case in the development of the modern tort of negligence. Let us now consider how a duty of care might arise. Imagine that Mark drives negligently and he omits to fix his broken brakes. In both instances he can reasonably foresee that he could injure someone and cause damage to their property. The persons to whom Mark owes a duty of care are those who would be closely and directly affected by Mark's negligent act of driving and the omission to repair the brakes, which he would understand to be his fellow motorists and pedestrians. The question of what is reasonably foreseeable is a question of fact and depends on the circumstances of the case.

In *Caparo Industries plc v Dickman* [1990] 2 AC 605, the House of Lords departed from the test established in *Anns v Merton LBC* [1978] 1 AC 728. Lord Bridge in *Caparo* established the modern test for determining whether a duty of care could arise in new situations. His Lordship held that:

> [I]n addition to the foreseeability of damage, necessary ingredients in any situation giving rise to a duty of care are that there should exist between the party owing the duty and the party to whom it is owed a relationship characterised by the law as one of 'proximity' or 'neighbourhood' and that the situation should be one in which the court considers it fair, just and reasonable that the law should impose a duty of a given scope upon the one party for the benefit of the other. (at pp. 617–618)

As part of determining whether there is a duty of care the court must ask whether it is 'fair, just and reasonable' to find that such a duty is owed. This goes beyond establishing factors such as reasonable foreseeability and proximity.

Pure economic loss

> ### Key definition: Pure economic loss
>
> This is a type of loss that is not consequential to personal injury or damage to property. It is purely concerned with having lost anticipated profits and as a general rule it is not recoverable.

As a general rule there is no duty of care to avoid causing pure economic loss. This is illustrated by the Court of Appeal's decision in *Spartan Steel & Alloys Ltd v Martin & Co (Contractors) Ltd* [1973] QB 27, where the court held that pure economic loss could not be recoverable as it was too remote. In this case an electricity cable had been negligently cut and this caused the claimant the following losses:

1   the metal, which was damaged as it was being processed at the time;
2   the loss of profits for that metal; and
3   loss of profits for the time that there was no power.

The first two losses were recoverable, even though the loss of profits for damaged metal was an economic loss, as it was consequential to the actual damage caused. However, the loss of profits during the time that production was halted was not recoverable as it was pure economic loss and therefore was not foreseeable. The decision was doubted by the House of Lords in *Junior Books Ltd v Veitchi Co Ltd* [1983] 1 AC 520. Their Lordships held that pure economic loss could be recovered where there was a sufficiently close relationship, i.e. proximity, between the parties and the duty of care that was owed could also cover non-foreseeable harm. However, the decision *Junior Books* has not always been followed by subsequent cases and it is of mixed judicial authority. It is clear that economic loss can be recovered if the loss is consequential to physical damage to property or it is caused as a result of personal injury (see *Leigh & Sullivan Ltd v Aliakmon Shipping Co Ltd* [1985] 2 AER 44).

Tort of deceit

We will now look at when the claimant is permitted to recover for pure economic loss where the loss has occurred as a result of the defendant being deceitful or fraudulent. The requirements needed in order for the defendant to be liable in deceit were reiterated in *Derry v Peek* (1889) 14 App Cas 337. Lord Herschell stated that the claimant must prove that the defendant was fraudulent. His Lordship observed that 'fraud is proved when it is shewn [shown] that a false representation has been made (1) knowingly, or (2) without belief in its truth, or (3) recklessly, careless whether it be true or false' (at p. 374). The defendant will be liable where it can be shown that he had no real honest belief in the truth of the statement. The defendant's motive is irrelevant. It is unsurprisingly very difficult to establish liability under the tort of deceit.

On-the-spot question

TSH Ltd holds an open day at its Bristol showroom to attract new clients. Damian owns House of Greeting Cards in Bath and asks one of TSH Ltd's directors why he should choose TSH Ltd to renovate his shop.

Damian is informed that TSH Ltd has a 100 per cent customer satisfaction rate. Based on the information that Damian has told him about his shop, the director informs Damian that the work should take no more than two weeks to complete. Damian is very impressed and enters into a contract with TSH Ltd. Later on he is annoyed to discover that the work took two months to complete and cost him an additional six weeks in lost sales. He has also discovered that TSH Ltd only has a 50 per cent customer satisfaction rate.

Advise Damian as to whether he can recover his loss of profits.

Negligent misstatement

The House of Lords in *Hedley Byrne & Co Ltd v Heller & Partners Ltd* [1964] AC 465 held that a duty of care could be owed to avoid causing pure economic loss by making a negligent misstatement.

KEY CASE ANALYSIS: *Hedley Byrne & Co Ltd v Heller & Partners Ltd* [1964] AC 465

Background

The claimant wished to place an order with a company. The claimant was personally liable for the orders placed and so asked the defendant, who was its banker, to make an inquiry into the company's finances. The defendant informed the claimant that the company's finances were fine. However, the defendant had included a disclaimer to exclude liability based on the advice that it had given the claimant. The information was incorrect.

Principle established

The House of Lords held that, where the defendant had made a negligent misstatement, a duty of care was owed to avoid causing the claimant pure economic loss. The defendant would be liable where he has made a negligent misstatement that could have been made honestly; he had been asked by the claimant to give advice or to provide specific information because of his special skills and the claimant actually had relied on the defendant's skill and judgment. The defendant must know or should have known that his advice would be relied upon. Importantly, while the burden of proof is still on the claimant, she does not need to establish that the defendant was fraudulent. Rather, she only needs to establish that the advice was given negligently.

However, in *Hedley Byrne* the defendant was not liable, despite a duty of care being owed, because the disclaimer prevented the defendant from being liable. This exclusion clause would now have to satisfy the requirement as to reasonableness under the Unfair Contract Terms Act 1977.

The assumption of responsibility by the maker of the written or oral statement is an important requirement in establishing liability for a negligent misstatement. In *IFE Fund SA v Goldman Sachs International* [2007] EWCA Civ 811 Waller LJ held that: 'The foundation for liability for negligent misstatements demonstrates that where the terms on which someone is prepared to give advice or make a statement negatives any assumption of responsibility, no duty of care will be owed' (at [28]). Nonetheless, the law can impose a duty if this can be established on the facts. The existence of a duty of care can be excluded by the parties' contract (see *Henderson v Merrett Syndicates Ltd (No 1)* [1995] 2 AC 145).

The advice must be given for a specific purpose and to an intended recipient. An example of when a duty of care will not arise was *Caparo Industries plc v Dickman* [1990] 2 AC 605.

KEY CASE ANALYSIS: *Caparo Industries plc v Dickman* [1990] 2 AC 605

Background

In *Caparo Industries plc v Dickman* [1990] 2 AC 605 the issue was whether a duty of care was owed for a negligent misstatement. The auditor had been instructed by company A to carry out a report on A's accounts. The report was negligent. The issue was whether Caparo Industries plc, the company that subsequently took over company A, could sue the auditors.

Principle established

The House of Lords held that liability for economic loss caused by a negligent misstatement would arise where a person makes a statement and communicates it to an intended recipient for a specific purpose, which was the reason that the maker understood her advice was given for. The recipient must have relied on the statement and have suffered a detriment. It was held that no duty of care was owed as the auditor had not intended or known that Caparo Industries plc would rely on its report when considering whether to take over company A.

Breach of duty

Not only must there be a duty of care but the defendant must have breached this duty. His conduct must fall below the standard expected from the reasonable person.

Causation

The claimant must prove that the defendant caused her loss. In *Barnett v Chelsea and Kensington Hospital Management* [1969] 1 QB 428, one of the issues to be determined was whether the defendant had caused the death of the claimant's husband. The claimant's husband had turned up at a hospital and informed the hospital that he was unwell. He was informed to go home and to see his own doctor in the morning. Unfortunately he died. The question was whether he would have died had he been treated that evening. The claim failed because it could not be proved that but for being turned away from the hospital he would not have died. We can see that for factual causation the but for test provides a way for the courts to determine whether the defendant's act or omission actually caused the claimant's loss.

On-the-spot question

? TSH Ltd is fitting out a shop in central London. One of TSH Ltd's labourers is bringing back coffees for his colleagues from a local café. As he is too busy concentrating on not spilling the coffee, he walks into TSH Ltd's scaffolding tower. The scaffolding tower collapses and blocks the road. Unfortunately, it damages three cars and shatters the windows of an upmarket tailoring shop, which causes shards of glass to fly everywhere and results in two of its employees suffering minor injuries. The police arrive five minutes later and decide to close the road for five hours. Upon being informed, TSH Ltd's managing director is grateful that the company took out insurance to cover this type of event. He immediately telephones the insurers and is shocked to be informed that the insurance policy he took out contains a number of exemptions and may prove insufficient. He is furious as he read an article in *Shop Fitters Weekly* that advised that this particular insurance policy covers all types of losses imaginable.

Discuss the above scenario in light of the liability that may arise in the tort of negligence.

Remoteness

The damages sought by the claimant must not be too remote. In *Overseas Tankship (UK) Ltd v Miller Steamship Co Pty Ltd (The Wagon Mound)* [1967] 1 AC 617, the Privy Council held that the risk of damage was not foreseeable and therefore the damages were too remote. In that case, due to the ship's engineer's negligence, oil had spilled into Sydney harbour and caused a fire. It is not enough that an event can be reasonably foreseen; the personal injury caused must itself be within the contemplation of a reasonable man (see *Bolton v Stone* [1951] AC 850).

Obvious danger

In *Tomlinson v Congleton BC* [2004] 1 A.C. 46, the House of Lords held that where the risk was clear to the claimant as there were clear warning signs that he ignored, then the defendant would not have breached the duty of care owed to the claimant as it was reasonable to expect the claimant to have taken steps to avoid the danger.

On-the-spot question

? TSH Ltd uses special clamps to attach its scaffold to the buildings it is working on. The clamps are over 15 years old and Fatima, TSH Ltd's area manager, is warned that there could be a risk that, as the clamps are old, they might damage the exterior of the building to which they are attached. Fatima does not think that the possible risk justifies the cost of replacing the clamps. Unfortunately, one afternoon Fatima is contacted by a colleague, who informs her that the clamps have caused the entire façade of a building to collapse.

Discuss TSH Ltd's possible liability in the tort of negligence.

TRESPASS TO THE PERSON

There can be liability in tort where a person has been falsely imprisoned, assaulted or suffers a battery. There is a crossover with the criminal law here. A business may face liability for trespass to the person where one of its employees physically assaults a customer. This is because the business as the employer could be vicariously liable.

PRIVATE NUISANCE

Key definition: Private nuisance

Liability arises where the defendant has unlawfully interfered with the claimant's enjoyment of her land.

A business could be liable in the tort of nuisance if it interferes with the claimant's enjoyment of his land. The claimant must have a right in the land (see *Hunter v Canary Wharf Ltd* [1997] AC 655 and *Newcastle-under-Lyme Corporation v Wolstanton Ltd* [1947] Ch 92). The claimant can sue for private nuisance where his enjoyment of the land is interfered with due to the defendant's unlawful interference. In order to prevent this interference, the claimant may ask the court to grant an injunction. Whether the claimant succeeds in establishing a cause of action for actionable private nuisance will depend on many factors. In *Sturges v Bridgman* (1879) 11 Ch D 852, the Court of Appeal held that whether some activity amounted to nuisance would depend on the location in which it took place. For businesses this is important, as a premise such as a factory or storage facility may cause frequent noise and if there is residential housing nearby there could be a risk that one of the residents will ultimately commence legal action. Other factors include the extent of and the duration of the alleged nuisance. The court will have to consider the reasonableness of the defendant's interference and the sensitivity of the claimant. The court will look at whether the claimant's enjoyment of the land relates to an ordinary use of the land, or if it is so sensitive that it will not amount to an actionable unlawful interference (see *Robinson v Kilvert* (1889) 41 Ch D 88).

Public interest

The court, in determining whether to grant an injunction to prevent the activity complained of from taking place, must weigh up the loss of enjoyment suffered by the claimant against the public interest in permitting the activity to take place.

KEY CASE ANALYSIS: *Miller v Jackson* [1977] QB 966

Background

In *Miller v Jackson* the claimant was unable to use their garden when cricket was being played on the adjacent green due to the risk of cricket balls falling into their garden. Cricket had been played on the green since the beginning of the twentieth century. The claimant had a house built adjacent to the green and the defendant had responded by building fences to try and prevent, albeit unsuccessfully, the cricket balls from landing on the claimant's property.

Principle established

The Court of Appeal held that the defendant's activity amounted to nuisance. However, it refused to grant an injunction to prevent cricket being played next to the claimant's property as it was held to be beneficial to the local youth.

In *Miller v Jackson*, Lord Denning MR disagreed with the majority that there was a nuisance:

> For over 70 years the game of cricket has been played on this ground to the great benefit of the community as a whole, and to the injury of none. No one could

suggest that it was a nuisance to the neighbouring owners simply because an enthusiastic batsman occasionally hit a ball out of the ground for six to the approval of the admiring onlookers. Then I would ask: Does it suddenly become a nuisance because one of the neighbours chooses to build a house on the very edge of the ground – in such a position that it may well be struck by the ball on the rare occasion when there is a hit for six? To my mind the answer is plainly No. The building of the house does not convert the playing of cricket into a nuisance when it was not so before.

The majority disagreed with Lord Denning MR and held that it was no defence for an action for nuisance for the defendant to argue that the claimant had chosen to move to an area where the activity, which the claimant regarded as a nuisance, had always taken place.

On-the-spot question

 Do you prefer the approach of Lord Denning or the majority in *Miller v Jackson* as to whether the defendant was liable for nuisance?

DEFAMATION

The law protects the reputation of individuals and businesses. In *South Hetton Coal Company Ltd v North-Eastern News Association Ltd* [1894] 1 QB 133, a company was able to recover damages where its reputation was injured by the defendant's libel. Libel refers to written statements and slander to oral statements that injure the claimant's reputation. Section 1(1) of the Defamation Act 2013 states 'A statement is not defamatory unless its publication has caused or is likely to cause serious harm to the reputation of the claimant'. Importantly, s.1(2) requires a business to establish that the published statement 'is likely to cause the body serious financial loss'. There are a number of defences available to the defendant, including the truth (s.2) and honest opinion (s.3).

OCCUPIERS' LIABILITY

Imagine that TSH Ltd own the freehold of its warehouse in Southampton and lease an office in Rochester. TSH Ltd would be the occupier of both premises and would be liable under the Occupiers' Liability Act 1957 to all visitors to its property. In *Wheat v E Lacon & Co Ltd*

[1966] AC 552, the House of Lords provided a definition of who was an occupier. Lord Denning held that an occupier, 'was simply a convenient word to denote a person who had a sufficient degree of control over premises to put him under a duty of care towards those who came lawfully onto the premises' (p. 577). Therefore, as TSH Ltd would have a sufficient degree of control over both premises it would be regarded as an occupier. The duty imposed by the Act is that of the 'common law duty of care' (s.2(1)). The extent of the duty owed depends on age of the visitors and special risks that visitors such as tradesmen would guard against (s.2(3)). The Occupiers Liability Act 1984 extends the liability of the occupier to include people who enter onto the occupier's land without permission.

PASSING OFF

Key definition: Passing off

A tort designed to protect the goodwill or reputation in goods that are manufactured or services that are provided by a business.

The tort of passing off protects the intellectual property in a business's name and the products it manufacturers. In *Reckitt & Colman Products Ltd v Borden Inc* (No 3) [1990] 1 WLR 491 Lord Oliver reiterated the requirements required for there to be an actionable passing off. The claimant is required to first, 'establish a goodwill or reputation attached to the goods or services which he supplies in the mind of the purchasing public'. This requires that the claimant prove that the product's distinctive feature generates goodwill, which equates to profits. Second, the claimant must 'demonstrate a misrepresentation by the defendant to the public (whether or not intentional) leading or likely to lead the public to believe that goods or services offered by him are the goods or services of the plaintiff'. A substantial number of the public must be confused and believe that the goods offered by the defendant are associated with those offered by the claimant. In *United Biscuits (UK) Ltd v Asda Stores Ltd* [1997] RPC 513, the supermarket chain Asda was selling chocolate biscuits and the packaging featured a puffin, which was similar to the 'Penguin' chocolate biscuit product manufactured by United Biscuits. Robert-Walker J was clear that, despite most customers realising that the products were different, 'many would believe that the two must be made by the same manufacturer'. The final requirement is that the claimant must demonstrate that:

> he suffers or . . . is likely to suffer damage by reason of the erroneous belief engendered by the defendant's misrepresentation that the source of the defendant's goods or services is the same as the source of those offered by the plaintiff.

The claimant has the burden of proof to establish that the defendant is liable. However, the tort of passing off is actionable, regardless of whether a distinctive feature of the product or its name is registered as a trade mark under the Trade Marks Act 1994.

INDUCING A BREACH OF CONTRACT

> ### Key definition: Inducing a breach of contract
>
> This is where the defendant knowingly induces another party to breach its contract with the claimant.

Imagine that A contracts with B. If B breaches the contract by refusing to perform her contractual obligations, then A can sue B for breach of contract. However, what if it was C who induces B to breach the contract? In this case A can sue C in tort for inducing the breach of contract. We can see that here tort is protecting the integrity of the contract between A and B. C may wish to induce B to breach a contract as he is seeking to obtain B's services or products. The tort of inducing a breach of contract was established in *Lumley v Gye* (1853) 2 E & B 216, where the court held that it was wrong that the person inducing the breach should escape liability. The defendant must intend to induce a breach and there is no need for the claimant to demonstrate that the defendant intended to cause her any damage. The tort was considered by the House of Lords in *OBG Ltd v Allan* [2008] 1 AC 1, where Lord Hoffmann reiterated the requirements needed for an actionable tort to occur:

> To be liable for inducing breach of contract, you must know that you are inducing a breach of contract. It is not enough that you know that you are procuring an act which, as a matter of law or construction of the contract, is a breach. You must actually realize that it will have this effect. Nor does it matter that you ought reasonably to have done so. (at [39])

The tort was treated as one of accessorial liability. You must intend to induce a breach. However, no liability will attach if the breach is 'merely a foreseeable consequence' (at [43]). The intention to induce a breach did not have to be motivated by malice.

This commonly arises where trade unions call for industrial action which means that trade union members breach their employment contracts by going out on strike. The Trade Union and Labour Relations (Consolidation) Act 1992 provides statutory protection for trade unions from being sued for inducing a breach of contract.

DEFECTIVE PRODUCT LIABILITY

The liability of a manufacturer of a product to the end user of the product was established in *Donoghue v Stevenson*. This permits the recovery of damages in tort regardless of whether the claimant had a contractual relationship with the defendant. The manufacturer will not be liable where the loss caused as a result of the product being defective is only pure economic loss. In *Murphy v Brentwood DC* [1991] 1 AC 398 Lord Keith stated that:

> [T]here is no liability in tort upon a manufacturer towards the purchaser from a retailer of an article which turns out to be useless or valueless through defects due to careless manufacture. The loss is economic. It is difficult to draw a distinction in principle between an article which is useless or valueless and one which suffers from a defect which would render it dangerous in use but which is discovered by the purchaser in time to avert any possibility of injury. (p. 465)

The decision in *Murphy* concerned whether the local authority was liable for negligently permitting the construction of houses on land that had been unsuitable and had caused subsidence. The House of Lords ruled that there was no liability as the claimants had suffered only pure economic loss. The manufacturer will be liable if its product causes physical damage or personal injury. In *D & F Estates v Church Commissioners* [1989] AC 177, Lord Bridge (at p. 478) discussed when liability might arise if a central heating boiler was defective. It is clear that the product, as a result of being defective, must damage other property. For example, if a boiler explodes and causes a fire, then any damage occurred to the building and its contents can be recovered. A defective product such as a house that suffers from subsidence will give rise to no liability if it just causes damage to itself.

Consumers have enhanced protection under the Consumer Protection Act 1987. The person who supplied the goods or the producer will not be liable where the product is defective and this causes only the product itself to be damaged (s.5(2)).

TORT OF CONVERSION

Key definition: Conversion

Occurs when there has been the use of a chattel by someone who does not own it, or does not have permission from its owner to use it. The use will be for an act inconsistent with the rights of the chattel's owner.

Lord Hoffmann in *OBG Ltd v Allan* [2008] 1 AC 1 observed that:

> Anyone who converts a chattel, that is to say, does an act inconsistent with the
> rights of the owner, however innocent he may be, is liable for the loss caused
> which, if the chattel has not been recovered by the owner, will usually be the
> value of the goods. (at [95])

The tort is one of strict liability. It is no defence to argue that you are an innocent purchaser
who purchased the chattel, i.e. personal property, in good faith (*Fowler v Hollins* (1872) LR 7
QB). The law protects the original owner of the property. We can see how the tort of
conversions works with reference to the decision in Chapter 4 on s.12 of the Sale of Goods
Act 1979. Liability for the conversion of goods has been put onto a statutory footing under
the Torts (Interference with Goods) Act 1977.

On-the-spot question

? TSH Ltd is looking to recruit a new managing director and its board of directors
decides to approach Liam Smith, the managing director of a rival company and
ask him if he would join TSH Ltd as its new managing director. Liam informs the
board of directors that contractually he must give his employer at least six months'
notice and therefore will not be able to join TSH Ltd before the six months have expired.
The board asks him to join TSH Ltd with immediate effect and to avoid giving any notice.
Liam agrees and picks up his work laptop and leaves to join TSH Ltd. Once at TSH Ltd's
premises he opens the laptop and sends an email to his employer saying that he is
resigning with immediate effect. Liam then starts working for TSH Ltd.

Discuss whether either TSH Ltd or Liam Smith is liable in tort?

SUMMARY

- If the requirements for the tort of negligent misstatement are met, then a business
  could be liable for causing pure economic loss.
- A business will be liable in tort if it induces the breach of a contract, interferes
  with goods owned by someone else, passes its goods or services off as being
  associated with another business, causes a private nuisance or where someone is
  injured at its premises.
- An employer is vicariously liable for the torts committed by its employees.

FURTHER READING

Buxton, R. 'How the common law gets made: *Hedley Byrne* and other cautionary tales' (2009) 125 *Law Quarterly Review* 60 – an interesting critique of how the common law has been developed by judges.

Deakin, S., Johnston, A. and Markesinis, B. *Markesinis and Deakin's Tort Law*, 7th edn (Oxford University Press, 2013) – refer to this textbook for a more in-depth discussion of the material covered in this chapter.

Hartshorne, J. 'Contemporary approaches towards pure economic loss in the law of negligence' (2014) 5 *Journal of Business Law* 425 – refer to this article for a discussion on the ability to recover pure economic loss.

Monaghan, C. 'When does imitation become passing off?' (2010) 31(6) *The Company Lawyer* 189 – refer to this short article for more detail on the tort of passing off.

Mullis, A. and Oliphant, K. *Torts*, 4th edn (Palgrave, 2011) – this is a clear and accessible textbook on tort law.

Chapter 6
The law of agency

LEARNING OBJECTIVES

After reading this chapter, you should be able to:

- appreciate the role of agency in facilitating business transactions;
- define agency and the different ways that an agency relationship can arise;
- understand the different types of authority that an agent may have;
- comprehend the difference between the disclosed and undisclosed principal; and
- appreciate the rights and duties of the agent.

INTRODUCTION

In this chapter we will explore what is meant by an agency and who are the parties in an agency relationship. We will look at how an agency is created and the types of authority that an agent can have. Surprisingly, an agent may exceed the actual authority given to him by the principal, the person who the agent is acting for, and therefore, the courts could still hold that the agent does have the authority to enter into a contract. This is non-consensual authority and we shall explore this as well as the consequences for the principal and agent where the agent exceeds his actual authority. We will look at the rights and duties of the agent and the consequences of the agent breaching the duties that he owes to the principal.

WHAT IS MEANT BY AGENCY?

An agency is where an individual or business, known as the agent, will work on behalf of another person or business, known as the principal and will represent the principal when dealing with third parties. There are many different types of agents, and one of the most common are estate agents, who advertise the principal's property for sale and will negotiate on behalf of their principal with third parties. Marketing agents will work for the principal and will establish a relationship with a third party, which will enable the principal to enter into a contract with the third party. However, a sales agent will enter into contracts with a third party on behalf of the principal. We can see that the agent is an essential part of business, as the principal will need individuals to act on its behalf. Academics have attempted to define agency and Roderick Munday has noted that '[t]he concept of agency is notoriously slippery and difficult to define', which is caused by the many different types of agency and the indiscriminate use of agency 'to describe individual and entities whose activities . . . are not actually governed by the law of agency' (*Agency: Law and Principles* (Oxford University Press, 2010), at [1.02]).

We can see that normally the principal and the agent will consensually enter into the agency relationship. This will be the case where the board of directors acting on behalf of the company (which is the principal) will in accordance to the articles of association appoint one of the directors to be the managing director. However, as we shall see, there will be times where the agency is non-consensual, such as where the agent exceeds the authority given to him by the principal.

An agent is a fiduciary and owes the principal fiduciary duties, as well as common law and contractual duties. The fact that the agent is a fiduciary emphasises the importance of the agent in his ability to enter into contracts with third parties which can alter the principal's legal position. Put simply, if you appoint an agent to act on your behalf, and even if you do not formally appoint them in that capacity, they could contract without authority to sell your property or compel you to purchase property from the third party. Potentially, the principal could be forced by the court to honour the contract.

THE PARTIES TO AN AGENCY CONTRACT

Key definition: Principal

The party for whom the agent acts. The agent will owe duties to the principal.

Key definition: Agent

The party who acts on behalf of the principal. The agent can be vested with the authority to enter into contracts on the principal's behalf.

Key definition: Third party

The party who has dealings with the agent and who the agent will contract with on behalf of the principal.

We shall see that there are three different relationships. First, we have the agency relationship between the principal and the agent. Here, there could be a contract between the agent and the principal, or indeed the agent's services could be provided free of charge. Second, there will be a relationship between the agent and the third party. We shall see that where the principal is disclosed (where the third party knows that there is a principal) then the agent will not be a party to the contract and will only facilitate the contract between the principal and third party. Finally, there is the contractual relationship between the principal and the third party.

THE FORMATION OF AN AGENCY RELATIONSHIP AND THE AUTHORITY OF THE AGENT

The agency relationship can be created in a number of ways. The principal could expressly appoint the agent or the agency could be implied from the fact that it is usual for a person in the agent's position to have the authority to enter into such a contract. In such cases the principal will have given his agent the actual authority to enter into that particular contract, based either on the express appointment and instructions given, or impliedly through the appointment of an individual to a particular position or task. Conversely, an agency can arise without the consent of the principal. We shall explore these non-consensual ways that create an agency and the agent's authority: apparent authority, usual authority and agency of necessity (Figure 6.1).

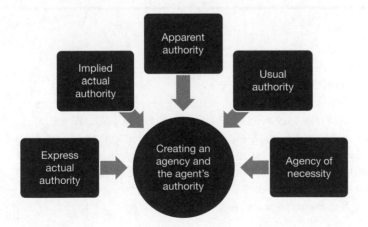

Figure 6.1 The different ways that an agent can have authority

> ### Key definition: Express actual authority
>
> Where an agent acts within the scope of the principal's express instructions.
>
> ### Key definition: Implied actual authority
>
> Where an agent acts in accordance with what is required to achieve the task given to him by the principal, or the agent acts within the scope of what is usual for someone in his position to do.
>
> ### Key definition: Apparent authority
>
> A form of estoppel based on whether the third party was led by the principal to believe that the agent had authority.
>
> ### Key definition: Usual authority
>
> A controversial form of authority based solely on what would be usual for an agent occupying the agent's position to do.
>
> ### Key definition: Agency of necessity
>
> Where the 'agent' is forced to take steps to look after the principal's property or to dispose of the principal's property in order to protect the principal's interest.

EXPRESS ACTUAL AUTHORITY

According to Lord Denning MR in *Hely-Hutchinson v Brayhead Ltd* [1968] 1 QB 549, the agent's authority, 'is *express* when it is given by express words, such as when a board of directors pass a resolution which authorises two of their number to sign cheques' (at p. 583). Therefore, if we were to appoint Josh as our agent and authorise him to conclude contracts up to the value of £12,000 on our behalf, then when Josh enters into such contracts he will be acting within the scope of his express actual authority. As Josh's principal we are bound to honour the contract.

Ambiguous instructions?

In *Ireland v Livingston* (1871–72) LR 5 HL 395 the House of Lords held that where the principal's instructions to the agent were ambiguous, the agent, so long as he acted honestly, would be held to be acting within the scope of his express actual authority. Devlin J in *Midland Bank Ltd v Seymour* [1955] 2 Lloyd's Rep 147, agreed with the reasoning given in *Ireland v Livingston*, that where the principal gives ambiguous instructions to the agent, and the 'agent acts upon [these] ambiguous instructions he is not in default if he can show that he adopted what was a reasonable meaning'. It was not open to challenge the agent's interpretation of the document as a whole. However, if it was clear that the instructions are ambiguous, then an agent would be expected to seek clarification from the principal. Robert Goff LJ in *European Asian Bank AG v Punjab & Sind Bank (No 2)* [1983] 1 WLR 642 observed:

> If instructions are given to an agent, it is understandable that he should expect to act on those instructions without more; but if, for example, the ambiguity is patent on the face of the document, it may well be right (especially with the facilities of modern communications available to him) to have his instructions clarified by his principal, if time permits, before acting upon them.

This approach was followed in *Cooper v National Westminster Bank plc* [2009] EWHC 3035 (QB), where it was held that the bank should have sought clarification from its client, and that proceeding without clarification was not reasonable in the circumstances.

IMPLIED ACTUAL AUTHORITY

If the agent has implied authority then he will be able to enter into contracts with a third party and the principal will be bound to honour these contracts. Implied actual authority can arise in a number of ways as was illustrated by the decision in *Hely-Hutchinson v Brayhead Ltd* [1968] 1 QB 549.

KEY CASE ANALYSIS: *Hely-Hutchinson v Brayhead Ltd* [1968] 1 QB 549

Background

Mr Richards was the chairman of the defendant company (the principal). The defendant wished to purchase the claimant's company. In order to keep the claimant's company from failing, the chairman promised in two separate letters that the defendant would indemnify the claimant for any personal guarantees that he gave to a third party. There was an offer of a £10,000 loan to cover the claimant's liability for the personal guarantee. Unfortunately, the claimant's business failed and the claimant was required to honour the personal guarantee. The claimant expected to be indemnified by the defendant. The defendant refused and argued that the claimant did not have the authority to give such an undertaking on behalf of the defendant. The defendant company's articles of association prohibited the chairman from acting in this way without the board's approval.

Principle established

The Court of Appeal held that the chairman of the defendant had the implied actual authority to promise to indemnify the claimant. Lord Denning MR held that:

> [actual authority] is *implied* when it is inferred from the conduct of the parties and the circumstances of the case, such as when the board of directors appoint one of their number to be managing director. They thereby impliedly authorise him to do all such things as fall within the usual scope of that office. (at p. 583)

Lord Denning MR held that the chairman did not have the express actual authority to offer the indemnity; this was because he was not authorised to do so by the defendant's articles of association. Neither did the chairman have the implied actual authority as a result of his position. This was because it was not usual for a chairman to make such an undertaking. However, the chairman had implied authority due to the fact that the defendant had permitted him to act as de facto managing director and had accepted the decisions that he had made in the past without requiring the prior authorisation of the board.

We can see from *Hely-Hutchinson* that authority can be implied where it is usual that someone occupying a particular position would be able to enter into certain types of contracts or to give certain undertakings. In *Hely-Hutchinson*, the chairman's authority did not emanate from his position, because it was not usual for a chairman to give such an undertaking. However, circumstances could suggest that a person would have such authority based on being allowed to make certain types of decisions in the past or unofficially occupying a position (as occurred in *Hely-Hutchinson*). We can see that the other directors had acquiesced in permitting the chairman to make unilateral decisions, so the chairman was acting within the scope of this implied actual authority. In *Industrie Chimiche Italia Centrale and Cerealfin SA v Alexander G Tsavliris & Sons Maritime Co (The Choko Star)* [1990] 1 Lloyd's Rep 516 the Court of Appeal was clear that 'implied actual authority of an agent extends to all subordinate acts which are necessary or ordinarily incidental to the exercise of his express authority.' This means that if we asked Phillipa to sell our house 'Greenacre', then Phillipa would have the implied actual authority to do everything that is incidental to achieve this. Therefore, Phillipa would be authorised to contract with estate agents, gardeners, removers and solicitors. We would be bound to honour these contracts, notwithstanding the absence of express authorisation. In *Rosenbaum v Belson* [1900] 2 Ch 267 the court held that an agreement instructed to sell a number of properties on behalf of the principal would have the authority to enter into a contract of sale without the express authority of the principal.

The limits of implied actual authority

If, however, there is a prohibition on what the agent may do and the agent exceeds this, then the agent cannot have implied actual authority. In *The Unique Mariner* [1978] 1 Lloyd's Rep 438, the court considered whether the master of a vessel could have the implied authority to bind the shipowner, and Brandon J observed that 'the implied actual authority of a master, unless restricted by such instructions lawfully given, extends to doing whatever is incidental to, or necessary for, the successful prosecution of the voyage and the safety and preservation of the ship.' Thus, while the scope of the ship's master, in his capacity as an agent extends to everything that is necessary and incidental to fulfilling what is expected from him, there are still limitations. The limitation is the existence of a prohibition that precluded him from acting in a particular way.

APPARENT AUTHORITY

Apparent authority, or ostensible authority, is based on the appearance of authority. As Lord Denning MR observed in *Hely-Hutchinson* 'apparent authority is the authority of an agent as it *appears* to others. It often coincides with actual authority (at p. 583)'. What does this mean? The answer is that apparent authority is a form of estoppel that operates to protect the third party. To illustrate how it works it is worth considering the following example:

- Rajah (the agent) works for Sandra (the principal) and Rajah has been informed that he does not have the authority to enter into contracts over £300 with the express approval of Sandra. If Rajah enters into a contract with Peter (the third party) which is over £300 and has not sought Sandra's permission, then Rajah is acting outside the scope of his express actual and implied actual authority. If Peter wished to enforce the contract against Sandra then she would argue that Rajah lacked authority and she would not be bound to honour the contract.
- However, if it appeared reasonable for Peter to believe that Rajah had the authority to enter into the contract, then apparent authority estops (prevents) Sandra from denying the contract. The question to determine is whether it was reasonable for the third party to believe that the agent had the authority to enter into contracts of that particular kind. We can see that apparent authority is based on what the third party reasonably believed and not what was said and done between the agent and the principal. If the agent did have the apparent authority and the principal does not fulfil the contractual obligations then the principal will be liable for breach of contract.

We can see that in the example above Rajah had:

- the actual authority to enter into contracts below £300; and
- the apparent authority to enter into a contract with Peter which was in excess of £300.

Sandra will argue that, while she consented to give Rajah the authority for the former, she did not consent for the latter. Apparent authority operates regardless of the consent of the principal.

Diplock LJ, in *Freeman and Lockyer v Buckhurst Park Properties (Mangal) Ltd* [1964] 2 QB 480, considered the relationship between actual and apparent authority and observed that '[they] are quite independent of one another. Generally they coexist and coincide, but either may exist without the other and their respective scopes may be different.'

In *Freeman and Lockyer*, Diplock LJ defined apparent authority as:

> [A] legal relationship between the principal and the contractor created by a representation, made by the principal to the contractor, intended to be and in fact acted upon by the contractor, that the agent has authority to enter on behalf of the principal into a contract of a kind within the scope of the 'apparent' authority, so as to render the principal liable to perform any obligations imposed upon him by such contract. To the relationship so created the agent is a stranger. (at p. 502)

We shall see that apparent authority is created by the principal's representation to the third party. The agent does not create apparent authority and he is indeed a stranger to the principal–third party relationship.

The requirements needed for apparent authority to exist

The requirements that are needed for the agent to have apparent authority have been established in a number of cases.

KEY CASE ANALYSIS: *Freeman and Lockyer v Buckhurst Park Properties (Mangal) Ltd* [1964] 2 QB 480

Background

Mr Kapoor and another individual formed a company (Buckhurst Park Properties) to purchase and resell land. Both men were appointed as directors. Mr Kapoor had agreed to pay for all the running expenses and the company in turn would reimburse him. Mr Kapoor entered into a contract with the claimant, Freeman and Lockyer, a firm of architects. The claimant sought repayment for their services from the defendant, Buckhurst Park Properties. The defendant denied that they owed the claimant any money as the contract had been entered into by Mr Kapoor personally and not on behalf of the company.

The Court of Appeal held that Mr Kapoor had apparent authority because although he was never officially appointed as managing director, he had been allowed by the defendant to act as if he were the managing director. It had appeared to the claimant that Mr Kapoor had been properly appointed as the managing director, and they were not required to find out before contracting with him whether he had actually been appointed to that position. Therefore, the defendant was liable.

Pearson LJ observed that:

In this case the company has known of and acquiesced in the agent professing to act on its behalf, and thereby impliedly representing that he has the company's authority to do so. The company is considered to have made the representation, or caused it to be made, or at any rate to be responsible for it. Accordingly, as against the other contracting party, who has altered his position in reliance on the representation, the company is estopped from denying the truth of the representation. (p. 498)

His Lordship held that a person relying on apparent authority is not required to have:

> [O]btained and studied the company's articles of association and the incorporated provisions of Table A and made sure that the directors had power to delegate to a single director. Such a requirement would be an absurd example of legal pettifoggery. (p. 500)

Diplock LJ considered the requirements that were needed for the court to find that the agent had apparent authority and therefore could enter into a contract without the consent of the principal.

Principle established

(1) that a representation that the agent had authority to enter on behalf of the company into a contract of the kind sought to be enforced was made to the contractor;

(2) that such representation was made by a person or persons who had 'actual' authority to manage the business of the company either generally or in respect of those matters to which the contract relates;

(3) that he (the contractor) was induced by such representation to enter into the contract, that is, that he in fact relied upon it (per Diplock LJ at p. 506).

1 There needs to be a representation to the third party

There needs to be a representation from the principal to the third party that the agent has authority. The representation cannot come from the agent, as Steyn LJ observed in *First Energy (UK) Ltd*: '[o]ur law does not recognise, in the context of apparent authority, the idea of a self-authorising agent.'

The question is how can the representation arise? The representation can be express or implied. A representation can arise when someone is appointed to a position that usually has the authority to enter into particular types of contracts. In *Armagas Ltd v Mundogas SA*, Lord Keith observed that 'when the principal has placed the agent in a position which in the outside world is generally regarded as carrying authority to enter into transactions of the kind in question' (at 777 B). However, the third party will not be able to establish that there was a representation where the agent was in a position that did not usually have the authority to enter into a transaction of that kind (see *Rama Corporation Ltd v Proved Tin & General Investments Ltd* [1952] 2 QB 147 and *British Bank of the Middle East v Sun Life Assurance Co of Canada* (UK) [1983] 2 Lloyd's Rep 9). The decision in *First Energy (UK) Ltd v Hungarian International Bank Ltd* [1993] Lloyd's Rep 194 illustrates how a representation can arise.

KEY CASE ANALYSIS: *First Energy (UK) Ltd v Hungarian International Bank Ltd* **[1993] Lloyd's Rep 194**

Background

First Energy supplied and installed heating systems and had created a scheme whereby customers would pay for the heating system over a period of time. To achieve this, First Energy required a credit facility and it approached the defendant. It negotiated with Mr Jamison, who was the senior manager for the defendant at its Manchester branch. The defendant, like many banks, distinguished between the internal authorisation of a credit facility and the authority to sign a letter announcing that the facility had been approved. The defendant required that two employees sign such a letter. However, the Court of Appeal observed that the claimant 'would not have been aware of the details of the internal hierarchy [and] . . . would only have been aware of the outward trappings of the office conferred on Mr Jamison by [the defendants]'. Crucially, Mr Jamison informed the claimant that he had no authority to sanction the credit facility. Subsequently, acting without the approval of the defendant Mr Jamison communicated to the claimant, via a facility letter, that a credit facility had been approved. The claimant sought to force the defendant to honour the credit facility offered in the letter.

Principle established

Steyn LJ observed that the court must protect 'the reasonable expectations of honest men' and that the court should avoid reaching a decision that would frustrate the 'reasonable expectations of the parties'. Steyn LJ held that the facility letter sent by Mr Jamison was capable of amounting to 'an unconditional and firm offer'.

Even though the claimant understood that Mr Jamison lacked the authority to authorise the credit facility, the fact that Mr Jamison was acting as a senior manager for the defendant meant that he had the apparent authority to send the facility letter containing a valid offer. Steyn LJ observed that while an agent cannot make a representation that he has the authority to enter into a particular transaction, he could still bind the principal through sending a letter that contained an offer that had been allegedly approved by his principal. This was as a consequence of the position that he held. Steyn LJ held that:

> Mr Jamison's position as senior manager in Manchester was such that he was clothed with ostensible authority to communicate that head office approval had been given for the facility set out in the 2nd August letter. Although his status was below that of a managing director or general manager, it was nevertheless considerable. And, in the circumstances of this case, the idea that First Energy should have checked with the managing director in London whether HIB had approved the transaction seems unreal.

To help explain the importance of the decision in *First Energy (UK) Ltd* we can see that:

- Mr Jamison was an agent and it appeared to the third party that he had considerable authority by virtue of his position;
- Mr Jamison did not have the authority (actual or apparent) to authorise the credit facility;
- Mr Jamison did have the authority (apparent) to communicate a purportedly valid offer of a credit facility on behalf of his principal.

First Energy (UK) Ltd is a controversial decision because of the ability of the agent to self-authorise the credit facility. However, we can see that in business it is usual for someone who is in a position of authority to be able to communicate legally binding offers, and it would be unrealistic for the third party to have to check with the principal.

Previous course of dealings

In *Summers v Solomon* (1857) 7 Ellis and Blackburn 879 a representation was created through the principal and third party's previous course of dealing. The agent had managed the principal's shop and had ordered goods from the third party which the principal had then paid for. The agent had then ordered goods on the principal's account and used these for himself. The court held that the principal was liable to pay the third party, because whatever the principal and agent had agreed privately as to the limits of the agent's authority this would not prevent the principal from being liable.

2 The representation must be from the principal or someone with the authority to make the representation

The representation must be from the principal or someone who has the authority to make the representation. In *Freeman and Lockyer* the representation was from the board of directors who had the authority to act on behalf of the principal. However, the representation must not come from the agent (*First Energy (UK) Ltd*).

3 The third party must rely on the representation

Apparent authority is a form of estoppel and the third party must rely on the representation. Not only must the third party not have actual notice that the agent lacks authority, he must not suspect that the agent lacks authority. This point was explained by Lord Scott in *Criterion Properties plc v Stratford UK Properties LLC* [2004] UKHL 28, [2004] 1 WLR 1846. Lord Scott observed that:

[I]f a person dealing with an agent knows or has reason to believe that the contract or transaction is contrary to the commercial interests of the agent's principal, it is likely to be very difficult for the person to assert with any credibility that he believed the agent did have actual authority. Lack of such a belief would be fatal to a claim that the agent had apparent authority. (at p. 1856)

The third party will not be able to argue that the agent has apparent authority where he should have known that the principal has made a public statement to limit the agent's authority. In *Overbrooke Estates Ltd v Glencombe Properties Ltd* [1974] 1 WLR 1335 the third party was held to have constructive notice because the auction particulars contain a limitation on the agent's authority. While reliance is required the third party need not suffer a detriment.

On-the-spot question

? Marcus works as the manager of Auto Trends, a car dealership, in London. He has recently been appointed as 'regional sales director' in recognition of his many years of service. Marcus has been informed by Auto Trends that his title is purely honorary and that he should still refer any issues such as discounts and credit facilities to head office.

On Monday, Roshan visits Auto Trends and wishes to purchase a car. He enquires about a discount and Marcus agrees to give him a 20 per cent discount. Roshan thinks that this is a very large discount, but having seen Marcus's name badge he proceeds to purchase the car.

On Tuesday, Amel visits Auto Trends and Marcus offers her a 10 per cent discount; he is wearing his name badge. Marcus heads back into his office and when he returns Amel agrees to purchase the car. On her way out Amel hears Marcus's colleagues discussing how he needs to have every decision approved by head office. Amel goes back into the showroom and Marcus informs her that he has contacted head office and they have approved the discount.

Discuss whether Marcus has authority to offer a 20 per cent discount.

USUAL AUTHORITY

> **Key definition: Disclosed principal**
>
> Where the principal is disclosed the third party will know that they are dealing with the agent in his capacity as an agent.
>
> **Key definition: Undisclosed principal**
>
> Where the principal is undisclosed the third party will be unaware of the principal's existence.

We have seen that the agent could have implied authority or apparent authority to bind the principal based on what was usual in terms of the authority a particular agency would have. This use of what is 'usual' is used along with other requirements to establish these types of authority. However, in *Watteau v Fenwick* [1893] 1 QB 346, it was held that an agent could have authority to bind the contract where he was acting without actual authority and there is no apparent authority, based solely on the usual authority of the position that he occupied.

KEY CASE ANALYSIS: *Watteau v Fenwick* [1893] 1 QB 346

Background

The principal employed a manager to run a pub. The manager's name was above the door and the licence was in his name. The manager had been expressly prohibited from purchasing certain types of goods. Nonetheless, he entered into a contract with a third party to purchase the prohibited goods. The goods were delivered on credit. The third party sought to recover the purchase price. Importantly, the principal was undisclosed, that is the third party never knew that the manager was acting as an agent, and believed that he was contracting with the manager in his own right.

Principle established

Clearly the agent did not have actual authority. Neither did he have apparent authority because there was no representation from the principal; this was due to the fact that the third party did not know that the principal existed. Wills J held that the agent could still have authority, as otherwise the 'secret limitation of authority would prevail and defeat the action of the person dealing with the agent and then discovering that he was an agent and had a principal'. To prevent 'mischievous consequences' the agent was held to have authority, because someone in his position would usually have such authority. Thus, usual authority was held to exist as an independent category of authority.

From a cursory reading of the case the decision in *Watteau v Fenwick* might not appear to be that controversial. Wills J was acting to protect the third party who did not know about the limitation. Had the principal been disclosed, that is known by the third party to exist, then the agent would have had apparent authority. However, Wills J gave the agent authority purely based on the usual authority of a pub manager. This negates the need for a representation to have been made by the principal. The decision was referred to in *Jerome v Bentley & Co* [1952] 2 All ER 114 and while the decision was not applied due to factual differences, the soundness of the decision was not questioned. However, in *Rhodian River Shipping Co SA v Halla Maritime Corp (The Rhodian River and The Rhodian Sailor)* [1984] 1 Lloyd's Rep 373, Bingham J doubted the decision in *Watteau v Fenwick* and noted that the decision had not been followed. Bingham J stated that he, 'would myself be extremely wary of applying this doctrine, if it exists . . .' There is considerable academic debate surrounding the decision in *Watteau v Fenwick* with academics criticising or defending the decision.

On-the-spot question

 Considering the comments made by Bingham J in *Rhodian River Shipping Co SA*, could it be said with some certainty that a third party will be unlikely to rely on *Watteau v Fenwick* today?

Discuss.

AGENCY OF NECESSITY

Another type of non-consensual agency is agency of necessity. This will operate where B is forced to take steps to look after P's property, or to dispose of P's property, in order to protect P's interest. Here P has not consented for B to deal with his property, or to incur expenses in looking after it. Nonetheless, the law operates to impose authority on B, as an agent of necessity, to deal with P's property or to recover expenses incurred. The decision in *Great Northern Railway Company v Swaffield* (1873–74) LR 9 Ex 132 illustrates how this occurs.

KEY CASE ANALYSIS: *Great Northern Railway Company v Swaffield* (1873–74) LR 9 Ex 132

Background

The defendant contracted with the claimant to transport the defendant's horse. When the horse arrived at its destination the defendant was not there to collect the horse. The claimant was forced to look after the horse and to contract with a stable to look after it. The claimant was able to recover the costs from the defendant. The court was aware that the claimant had a duty to look after the horse and therefore it would be wrong not to permit him to recover the additional costs.

Principle established

Pollock B cited the decision of *Cargo ex Argos (No 2)* (1872–75) LR 4 A & E 13, where the court had held:

> [N]ot merely is a power given, but a duty [is] cast on the master, in many cases of accident and emergency, to act for the safety of the cargo in such manner as may be best under the circumstances in which it may be placed; and that, as a correlative right, he is entitled to charge its owner with the expenses properly incurred in so doing. (at p. 164)

This had been developed within the context of carrying goods by sea and was extended in *Great Northern Railway Company* to apply to a contract for rail carriage. Therefore, the claimant could recover as an agent of necessity.

It has been doubted whether *Cargo ex Argos* and *Great Northern Railway Company* are cases where an agency of necessity had arisen. The decisions could be explained under the law of bailment, where a party in possession of the goods has the responsibility to look after these and thus can recover his expenses. Lord Diplock in *Pacific SA v Food Corp of India (The Winson)* [1982] AC 939 believed that the cases could be explained this way. In *Petroleo Brasileiro SA v ENE Kos 1 Limited* [2012] UKSC 17, Lord Sumption observed that in *Great Northern Railway Company* there had been no emergency (which is now required for an agency of necessity to arise) and the claimant could have recovered his losses under the law of bailment.

Key definition: Bailment

Where a person receives good (from the bailor) into his possession whether consensually (or sometimes non-consensually) he becomes a bailee and must look after these goods until he returns the goods to the bailor, or is directed by the bailor to give the goods to a third party.

RATIFICATION

Where the agent has acted without authority, the principal can ratify the contract and accept it as his own contract. However, in order to ratify the contract, the principal must have been inexistence at the time when the contract was made (*Kelner v Baxter* (1866–67) LR 2 CP 174). This permits the principal to enforce the contract against the third party. If the agent acts without authority and the principal subsequently ratifies the contract, then the principal will be bound to honour the contract (see *New Falmouth Resorts Ltd v International Hotels Jamaica Ltd* [2013] UKPC 11).

THE DISCLOSED AND UNDISCLOSED PRINCIPAL

We have seen that the principal can be disclosed and undisclosed. Where the principal is undisclosed the third party believes that the agent is the other party to the contract. The third party does not realise that the agent is contracting on behalf of the undisclosed principal. This means that if, and when, the undisclosed principal intervenes and seeks to enforce the contract, the third party might be unhappy that the undisclosed principal is now a party to the contract. The undisclosed principal is an exception to the doctrine of privity and enables the principal to intervene on the contract as a party in his own right.

This could be viewed as unfair to the third party and the question is why does the law permit the undisclosed principal to intervene. In *Keighley, Maxsted & Co v Durrant* [1901] AC 240, Lord Lindley explains the justification for this:

> [T]here is an anomaly in holding one person bound to another of whom he knows nothing and with whom he did not, in fact, intend to contract. But middlemen, through whom contracts are made, are common and useful in business transactions, and in the great mass of contracts it is a matter of indifference to either party whether there is an undisclosed principal or not.
> (p. 261)

However, third parties are not always indifferent. In *Said v Butt* [1920] 3 KB 497, the third party successfully excluded the undisclosed principal from the contract.

KEY CASE ANALYSIS: *Said v Butt* [1920] 3 KB 497

Background

The claimant had made unfounded allegations against the defendant's theatre. The claimant wished to attend a play at the defendant's theatre and twice applied for tickets in his own name. Twice his request was refused. He asked his friend to purchase tickets in his name. The tickets were purchased and the claimant turned up with his ticket and sought entry. Unsurprisingly, he was refused entry by the defendant and sued for breach of contract.

Principle established

The claimant was an undisclosed principal and his friend had acted as an agent. However, the court held that because the identity of the parties was a material consideration there was not a contract that the claimant could enforce. It was clear that the defendant would never have contracted with the claimant.

The decision in *Said v Butt* is controversial. In *Dyster v Randall & Sons* [1926] Ch 932, the third party was unsuccessful in excluding the undisclosed principal from the contract. While the undisclosed principal knew that the third party would never have sold the land to him, the personal identity of the purchaser was not a material ingredient to the contract. This means that the third party was not contracting with the purchaser because of some particular personal characteristic, as it was simply a sale of land. The fact that the agent did not reveal that he was only an agent did not amount to a misrepresentation. Consequently, the undisclosed principal could enforce the contract. In *Rolls Royce Power Engineering plc v Ricardo Consulting Engineers Ltd* [2003] EWHC 2871 (TCC), the third party was able to exclude the undisclosed principal because of the fact that the personal characteristics of the parties was a material consideration. This was because the third party and the agent's employees had a good working relationship and this was a material consideration.

On-the-spot question

? Alison owns two coffee shops in the centre of Leeds. She wishes to sell one of the coffee shops and is approached by Henry who is a potential purchaser. After agreeing to sell the coffee shop, Alison discovers that Henry was acting for her former husband, William, who had previously offered to purchase the coffee shop and she had refused to sell it to him.

Advise Alison as to whether she can exclude William from the contract.

THE RELATIONSHIP BETWEEN THE THIRD PARTY AND THE AGENT

Where the principal is disclosed the third party cannot usually sue the agent for breach of contract, as the agent was not a party to the contract. If the agent is acting without authority (actual or other) the third party is then entitled to sue the agent for breach of his collateral warranty of authority (see *Collen v Wright* (1857) 7 E & B 647). This is because the agent, when contracting with the third party, has warranted that he is acting with authority. The warranty of authority could also be made to someone else other than the third party (see *Penn v Bristol & West Building Society* [1997] 1 WLR 1356).

If, however, the principal is undisclosed, the agent is a party to the contract. The contract is initially between the agent and third party. Both are capable of being sued by or suing the other (see *Sims v Bond* (1833) 5 B & Ad 389). Once the principal chooses to intervene, the third party can choose to sue either the principal or the agent. The third party cannot sue both; therefore he must elect who to sue and once he obtains judgment against either the principal or the agent, the claims merge and he can no longer sue the other (see *Kendall v Hamilton* (1879) 4 App Cas 504). Finally, where the undisclosed principal has intervened in the contract, the agent will remain liable to the third party. However, the agent cannot sue the third party.

THE RIGHTS OF THE AGENT

At common law the agent has a number of rights against the principal in addition to any rights contained in the contract between them.

The agent is entitled to be indemnified for any legitimate expenses or any liabilities incurred while acting within the scope of his authority. The agent can exercise a lien over the principal's goods if he has not been paid any money by the principal. The lien only applies to the goods in the agent's possession that relate to the agency (*Taylor v Robinson* (1818) 8 Taunt 648). The lien can be excluded expressly or by implication in the contract (*Withers LLP v Langbar International Ltd* [2011] EWCA Civ 1419).

The agent can receive either commission or remuneration. The method of payment will often be determined by the agency contract. If the agent is to be paid commission, then the agent must actually bring about the commissionable event. If the agent is tasked with finding a purchaser and he does this, then the agent will not receive commission unless the sale takes place. The courts will not imply a term into the agency contract to force the principal to sell the property so that the agent has an opportunity to earn his commission (*Luxor (Eastbourne) Ltd v Cooper* [1941] AC 108). If the contract is silent as to remuneration the courts may imply a term where the work provided by the agent would have been performed with the expectation of remuneration (*Way v Latilla* [1937] 3 All ER 759).

DUTIES OF THE AGENT

In addition to the duties in the agency contract, the agent owes the principal a number of important duties. The agent must act with reasonable skill and care and act within the scope of his actual authority. The agent cannot delegate his duties without the consent of the principal. The agent is also a fiduciary and therefore owes fiduciary duties to his principal. This creates a relationship of trust and confidence. These duties protect the principal, as the agent will potentially have the power to deal with the principal's property and act on his behalf. Not all agents will owe the same duties or to the same extent (*Kelly Cooper* [1993] AC 205).

KEY CASE ANALYSIS: *Kelly v Cooper* [1993] AC 205

Background

Kelly approached Cooper, an estate agent, to find a purchaser for his property. Kelly's neighbour Brant was also looking to sell his property. A third party called Perot wished to purchase both properties in order to redevelop the land. Cooper was acting for both Kelly and Brant and arranged for Perot to purchase both properties. Neither Kelly or Brant knew about this, or that Perot was purchasing the neighbouring property. Kelly sued Cooper for breach of his fiduciary duties as Cooper had failed to disclose important information and had created a situation where there was a conflict of interest between disclosing information to the principal and earning commission on both houses.

Principle established

The case was decided by the Privy Council and Lord Browne-Wilkinson accepted that the third party's interest in purchasing both properties was important as, had Kelly known this during negotiations, he could have used this to his advantage. However, Cooper was an estate agent and not all types of agents owed the same duties and these could be impliedly excluded. Both sellers would have realised that Cooper would act for other parties and that they could not expect full disclosure as 'otherwise [estate agents] will be unable to perform their function'. The decision was criticised by Professor Reynolds as seeming 'to deny fiduciary obligations to all and to leave everything to express and implied terms of the contract' ([1994] JBL 144 at 149).

The decision in *Kelly v Cooper* was cited approvingly by the House of Lords in *Hillier v Barker Booth & Edward* [2008] UKHL 8. We can see that in *Kelly v Cooper* the duties where modified by implication. It is also possible to exclude the duties in the contract, although this exclusion will be subject to the Unfair Contract Terms Act 1977.

On-the-spot question

? Given the importance of knowing that a prospective purchaser wishes to purchase the neighbouring property, in order to secure a higher purchase price, could it be argued that the decision in *Kelly v Cooper* undermines the duties that an agent owes his principal?

Discuss.

The agent as a fiduciary must not act to create an actual or potential conflict of interest between his own (or a third party's) interest and the interest of his principal. According to *Chitty on Contracts* (31st edn), the agent 'owes fiduciary duties to prefer his principal's interests to his own'. In *Aberdeen Rly Co v Blaikie Bros* (1854) 1 Macq 461, Lord Carnworth LC stated:

> It is a rule of universal application that no one, having [fiduciary] duties to discharge, shall be allowed to enter into engagements in which he has, or can have, a personal interest conflicting, or which may possibly conflict, with the interests of those whom he is bound to protect (at p. 471).

So what if the agent wishes to pursue an activity that might create a conflict of interest? The answer is that the agent must seek the principal's consent. The agent must not use the principal's property or information, which he learns while acting for the principal for his own benefit (*Boardman v Phipps* [1967] 2 AC 46). The agent must not take bribes or make a secret commission (see the recent decision of the Supreme Court in *FHR European Ventures LLP and others v Cedar Capital Partners LLC* [2014] UKSC 45). The agent must be financially accountable to the principal and keep their funds separate and the accounts open for inspection. The agent must also act in the best interests of the principal and reveal all relevant information.

If the agent breaches any of his duties he could lose his right to commission or have his agency terminated (*Boston Deep Sea Fishing & Ice Co v Ansell* (1888) LR 39 Ch D 339). Not every breach of a duty, even a fiduciary duty, will mean that the agent will lose his commission. In *Kelly v Cooper*, Lord Browne-Wilkinson observed that an agent should only lose the right to commission where the breach of fiduciary duties was dishonesty, or if honest, the breach went to the root of the agent's obligations. In *Hippisley v Knee Bros* [1905] 1 KB 1 it had been decided that an agent would only lose the right if the commission was not fraudulent or dishonest, or connected to the contract that he performed on behalf of the principal (per Lord Alverstone CJ at 8).

THE COMMERCIAL AGENTS (COUNCIL DIRECTIVE) REGULATIONS 1993/3053

We have seen that the agent has very few rights against his principal when these are contrasted with the duties that he owes the principal. The Commercial Agents (Council Directive) Regulations 1993/3053 have introduced new rights and duties. This only applies to commercial agents (see regulation 2). The commercial agent is protected in a number of ways, including the entitlement to commission during and after the termination of the agency (regulations 7–9). When the principal wishes to terminate an agency there is a minimum notice requirement (regulation 15). There is also an automatic entitlement for the agent to be compensated upon the termination of the agency, or to be indemnified if the contract states otherwise (regulations 17–18).

TERMINATION OF THE AGENCY

The agency can be terminated in accordance to the contract, the common law and the Commercial Agent (Council Directive) Regulations.

SUMMARY

- An agent can have both consensual and non-consensual authority, which permits him to enter into contracts on behalf of the principal.
- Apparent authority is based on the appearance of authority and requires a representation from the principal to the third party.
- The undisclosed principal is an anomaly in the law of contract and permits the principal to intervene on a contract made by his agent.

FURTHER READING

Brown, I. 'The agent's apparent authority: paradigm or paradox' [1995] *Journal of Business Law* 360 – this article explores the decision in *First Energy (UK) Ltd* and the circumstances where an agent can have apparent authority.

Cheng-Han, T. 'Undisclosed principals and contract' (2004) *Law Quarterly Review* 480 – this article explores the justification for permitting the undisclosed principal.

Goodhart, A. L. and Hamson, C. J. 'Undisclosed principals in contract' (1930–32) *Cambridge Law Journal* 320 – this article is about the undisclosed principal and discusses the rationale for permitting the principal to remain undisclosed.

Reynolds, F. M. B. 'Breach of warranty of authority: a point elucidated' [1998] *Journal of Business Law* 151 – this is an interesting commentary on the decision in *Penn v Bristol & West Building Society* [1997] and the author discusses the requirements for a warranty of authority to exist.

Roderick, M. *Agency: Law and Principles*, 2nd edn (Oxford University Press, 2013) – this book is a thorough and thoughtful consideration on the law of agency. It is written in an accessible manner and will give you more detailed analysis of the material covered in this chapter.

Tettenborn, A. 'Agents, business owners and estoppel' (1998) *Cambridge Law Journal* 274 – this article is concerned with apparent authority.

Chapter 7
Employment law

LEARNING OBJECTIVES

After reading this chapter, you should be able to:

- appreciate the legal responsibilities of an employer to their employees;
- define what is meant by the term employee and who is considered to be a employee;
- understand the claims that an employee can have against their employer upon the termination of their contract;
- comprehend what is meant by a restrictive covenant, a garden leave clause and the implied duty of fidelity; and
- appreciate the protection offered to employees by the Equality Act 2010.

INTRODUCTION

Most businesses will employ people and therefore it is important that those who are responsible for recruiting, dismissing and managing employees understand how employment law operates. Everyone who reads this chapter will at some stage of their careers be an employee, or perhaps will be responsible for managing others and recruiting new employees. Employment law is a fascinating area of law and is highly relevant to businesses and individuals. We shall see in this chapter that an employer is restricted as to how and in what circumstances they can dismiss an employee, that they must also ensure that their recruitment and working practices do not discriminate and that they comply with various legal requirements such as the Working Time Regulations, the National Minimum Wage Act 1998, health and safety, and parental rights. Employment law requires reference to and familiarity with statutory provisions and these can be accessed freely at www.legislation.gov. uk. It is recommended that you refer to these important provisions throughout the chapter.

Employment law is complex and this chapter is only intended as an introduction. Therefore, it is essential that you refer to the further reading to help develop your knowledge of this interesting and highly relevant subject. Employment law is undergoing considerable reform, as the Coalition government is keen to encourage businesses to recruit and have removed some of the problems that are associated with employing individuals.

The Beecroft Report which was published in 2012 recommended radical changes and proved to be very controversial. The report was not an official government report and was carried out by Mr Adrian Beecroft, who is a private individual. Many of the recommendations made in the report were rejected or implemented as a result of the existing Employment Law Review. The Enterprise and Regulatory Reform Act 2013 and the Growth and Infrastructure Act 2013 have introduced some important changes that you will need to be aware of. These include:

- changes to unfair dismissal;
- changes to redundancy;
- creation of the employee shareholder.

EMPLOYMENT STATUS

It is important to appreciate that there is a hierarchy in terms of employment law rights. Statutory provisions offer the employee considerably more protection than those individuals classified as workers or who are genuinely self-employed.

Whether an individual will be an employee is not always straightforward and will involve looking at a number of factors. It is important to note that an employee enjoys a privileged legal status and has enhanced rights when compared to those persons classified as workers:

- An employee will enjoy the right not to be unfairly dismissed or to be made redundant, whereas a worker does not enjoy these statutory rights.
- However, both an employee and a worker are protected against wrongful dismissal and must be paid no less than the national minimum wage.

Example

You may have entered into a contract to work for another but that does not necessarily mean you will be an employee. Consider this example: Linda is employed by Delby Ltd to run its accounts department. Linda is an employee and has a continuous contract of employment. During the Christmas period an agency worker assists Linda. The agency worker is hired from an agency that supplies administrative support. The agency worker is not an employee of Delby Ltd (we shall see why below). Delby Ltd has also hired Rupert on a casual basis over the Christmas period. Rupert is not an employee but rather he is a worker (we shall also see why below).

This does not mean that the agency worker does not have any rights against Delby Ltd. Agency workers have received increased rights under the Agency Workers Regulations 2010 (SI 2010/93).

So how would we determine whether an individual is an employee?

Key definition: A contract of employment

A contract of employment is defined by s.230 (2) Employment Rights Act 1996 (ERA 1996): 'In this Act "contract of employment" means a contract of service or apprenticeship, whether express or implied, and (if it is express) whether oral or in writing.'

Looking at the definition above, we can see that a contract of employment can be:

- a contract of service, and not a contract for services;
- implied or express;
- expressly made orally or in writing.

In order to determine whether we have an employment contract, a useful starting place is the employment contract. However, the contract is not conclusive, as the courts will disregard contracts that state that an individual is not an employee, where such a description is a sham. The Court of Appeal in *Protectacoat Firthglow Ltd v Szilagyi* [2009] EWCA Civ 98 held that in determining whether a contract was a sham the court should consider whether the words used actually reflected the parties' true expectations or intentions.

Key definition: Employee

Section 230 (1) ERA 1996 provides a statutory definition of an employee: 'In this Act "employee" means an individual who has entered into or works under (or, where the employment has ceased, worked under) a contract of employment.'

The definition from s.230 ERA 1996 is not particularly helpful and the common law has developed a number of tests to determine employment status. The older tests focused on how much control the employer had over the individual, or how integrated an individual was within the employer's organisation (per Denning LJ in *Bank voor Handel en Scheepvaart N. V. Slatford* [1953] 1 QB 248).

The multiple or economic reality test

The test that is used today is the multiple test (or as it is otherwise known, the economic reality test). The test is so called because the courts will consider a number of criteria in order to see whether an individual is an employee. The test is from *Ready Mixed Concrete (South East) Ltd v Minister of Pensions and National Insurance* [1968] 2 QB 497.

KEY CASE ANALYSIS: *Ready Mixed Concrete (South East) Ltd v Minister of Pensions and National Insurance* **[1968] 2 QB 497**

Background

A company entered into a contract with Mr Latimer. In the contract he was described as an independent contractor. Mr Latimer owned the vehicle that he used for company business and he was paid for every mile that he used the vehicle for company business. The vehicle was required for the exclusive use of the company and this meant that he could not work for anyone else. Mr Latimer was able to provide a substitute driver as long as the company consented to this. He had to comply with the company rules, wear the company uniform and pay his own income tax and national insurance. The question which had to be determined by the court was whether Mr Latimer was an employee.

Principle established

Mackenna J held that there were three conditions that had to be fulfilled in order for a contract of service to exist:

(i)   The servant agrees that, in consideration of a wage or other remuneration, he will provide his own work and skill in the performance of some service for his master.

(ii) He agrees, expressly or impliedly, that in the performance of that service he will be subject to the other's control in a sufficient degree to make that other master.

(iii) The other provisions of the contract are consistent with its being a contract of service (at p. 515).

Mr Latimer was held not to be an employee: 'A man does not cease to run a business on his own account because he agrees to run it efficiently or to accept another's superintendence' (at p. 526).

The fact that he enjoyed sufficient freedom meant that he was an independent contractor and not an employee:

He is free to decide whether he will maintain the vehicle by his own labour or that of another, and, if he decides to use another's, he is free to choose whom he will employ and on what terms. He is free to use another's services to drive the vehicle when he is away because of sickness or holidays, or indeed at any other time when he has not been directed to drive himself. He is free again in his choice of a competent driver to take his place at these times, and whoever he appoints will be his servant and not the company's. (at p. 526)

Mackenna J observed that the judge must determine the classification of the contract. The fact that someone may be under an obligation to perform work and agree to be under another's control 'is a necessary, though not always a sufficient, condition of a contract of service' (at p. 517). However, Mackenna J was of the opinion that degree of control was not everything or the only factor to consider.

In *Market Investigations Ltd v Minister of Social Security* [1969] 2 QB 173, Cooke J considered the tests that are used to determine whether there was a contract of service or a contract for service. Cooke J (at pp. 184–185) noted that it might not be possible to draw an exhaustive list of the factors which the court would consider. He noted that 'control will no doubt always have to be considered, although it can no longer be regarded as the sole determining factor' and that important factors included:

- whether the person supplies his own equipment;
- whether the person hires his own workers;
- the extent of his financial risk and the opportunity for profit;
- the responsibility for investment and management.

Sometimes it will be straightforward to ascertain whether an individual will, or will not, be an employee. However, it can be quite difficult, especially if an individual is permitted to allow another person to perform his work or to refuse to work a particular shift. A number of factors must be considered in determining whether a person is an employee. We have seen that where there is sufficient independence there will not be a contract of service.

Mutuality of obligations and personal service

The mutuality of obligations is required for there to be a contract of service. This means that the employer must be under an obligation to provide work and the employee must be under an obligation to accept it. In *Ready Mixed Concrete* the ability to substitute was held to be inconsistent with a contract of service. In *Express & Echo Publications Ltd v Tanton* [1999] ICR 693, Peter Gibson LJ stated:

> [I]t is necessary for a contract of employment to contain an obligation on the part of the employee to provide his services personally. Without such an irreducible minimum of obligation, it cannot be said that the contract is one of service.
> (at p. 699)

In *Express & Echo Publications Ltd* a delivery driver was held to be an independent contractor as he was permitted to engage a substitute driver at his own expense. Thus the employee must perform personal service. The House of Lords in *Carmichael v National Power Plc* [1999] 1 WLR 2042 held that tour guides who were employed at a power plant on a casual basis were not employees as there was no mutuality of obligations. The tour guides were only asked to work when the employer required them to. The House of Lords rejected the Court of Appeal's approach. The Court of Appeal had found an implied term that there was an obligation that a reasonable amount of work would be offered and performed (see *Carmichael v National Power plc* [1998] IRLR 301). The ability to turn down work can indicate that you are not an employee. If you are able to choose whether to work on any particular day, and if you do not choose to work then someone else will perform the work, you will not be an employee (*Bebbington v Palmer (t/a Sturry News)* [2010] UKEAT/0371/09/DM).

Even if you are able to delegate your work to someone else, you could still be an employee. This was the case in *Weight Watchers (UK) Ltd v Revenue and Customs Commissioners* [2010] UKFTT 54 (TC), where it was held that there was a strong degree of control by Weight Watchers over people running the weight loss groups and that there existed the mutuality of obligations, notwithstanding the ability of the employees to delegate their meetings to other persons. This was because their freedom of nomination was restricted to other group leaders and they receive no monetary consideration for these meetings. This decision is similar to *MacFarlane v Glasgow City Council* [2001] IRLR 7 where the right to delegate was controlled by the employer. In *Autoclenz Ltd v Belcher* [2011] UKSC 41; [2011] ICR 1157, the Supreme Court considered whether car valeters were employees.

KEY CASE ANALYSIS: *Autoclenz Ltd v Belcher* [2011] UKSC 41; [2011] ICR 1157

Background

The case concerned car valeters who worked for a company that required them to sign a contract stating that they were not employees. The contract also contained other terms that were inconsistent with this being a contract of service. The car valeters brought a claim submitting that they were workers for the purpose of the Working Time Regulations 1999 and the National Minimum Wage Regulations 1999.

Principle established

The Supreme Court held that they were workers for the purposes of the claim, and that they were employees. It was possible to disregard the written contract if it was inconsistent with the parties' actual relationship. The court held that the right to substitute your work to another was inconsistent with a person being an employee. Even if such a clause was not used, its existence would still prevent someone from being an employee. However, this was the case only if such a clause was genuine and reflected the parties' true intentions. If it did not do this, then the court may disregard the clause (see *Protectacoat Firthglow Ltd v Szilagyi* above). The court would need to consider the parties' relative bargaining power to determine whether the parties' agreement was a sham, i.e. is the employer in a dominant position? In Autoclenz the Supreme Court disregarded the written contract and the substitution clause.

Now let us consider whether Horace would be regarded as an employee:

On-the-spot question

? Horace works for Delby Ltd's private tuition department. He works 35 hours a week. His contract states that he is self-employed and responsible for paying his own income tax and national insurance. Horace is required to work Monday to Friday from 9.00am to 5.00pm. His contract permits him to delegate his teaching to colleagues and lecturers from other institutions, so long as they are on Delby Ltd's list of approved tutors.

Would Horace be considered to be an employee?

Agency workers

In *James v Greenwich London Borough Council* [2007] ICR 577, the question to be determined was whether an agency worker could be an employee of the end user. The end user will have a contract with the agency, which will then supply the agency worker. The Court of Appeal held that the fact the agency worker had worked for the end user for a long time was not enough to establish a contract of employment. The key issue was whether there was an implied contract, which was inconsistent with there being no contract. The Court of Appeal had agreed with the tribunal that where there was an agency relationship, there was no need to imply a contract.

Employee shareholders

You should be aware that the new employee shareholder status will apply to those employees who agree to exchange many of their employment rights in return for shares in their employer's business (see the Growth and Infrastructure Act 2013). This has proved very controversial because, for as little as £2,000 worth of shares, it is possible for an employer to remove a considerable amount of the statutory protection that is currently afforded to employees.

THE EMPLOYMENT CONTRACT

As we have seen, the word 'employee' is just descriptive. The agreement could amount to a sham, as it does not reflect the actual operation of the contract.

Written statement

There is no requirement that the contract must be in writing (s.230(2) ERA 1996). All that is required is that the employee receives a written statement of particulars under s.1 ERA 1996. This must be given to the employee not less than two months after the beginning of the employment (s.1(2) ERA 1996). The statement needs to contain information including the names of the employer and the employee, the rate of pay or how pay will be calculated, terms relating to hours of work, the job title, and description of the work that the employee will perform.

Terms

The terms in the contract can be express or implied. Terms can be implied through a number of tests such as the business efficacy test, the officious bystander test and to reflect industry practice. Terms can also be potentially incorporated into a contract through a collective agreement that has been agreed between the employer and the employees' trade union. Throughout this chapter we will see examples of implied terms.

VARIATION OF THE CONTRACT

The employer may wish to vary the contract for a number of reasons. The general rule is that the employer may not vary the contract unilaterally; however, the employer could include a clause that will permit a variation without requiring the employees' consent (see *Wandsworth v London Borough Council v D'Silva* [1998] IRLR 193). In *Bateman v Asda Stores Ltd* [2010] IRLR 370 the staff handbook was part of the contract and it contained a right for the employer to change the terms of contract. The clause was clear and unambiguous. The employer unilaterally introduced a new pay structure and this was held not to amount to a breach of contract. However, a unilateral variation of the contract without such a clause could amount to a repudiatory breach of the contract.

BUSINESS TRANSFERS

If the employer transfers the whole or part of the business, then the Transfer of Undertakings (Protection of Employment) (TUPE) Regulations 2006 will apply. TUPE protects the employees and protects their existing contractual rights.

VICARIOUS LIABILITY

The employer will be liable for the torts that an employee commits in the course of their employment. The employer will not be liable where the employee is held to be acting outside the scope of their employment (see *Rose v Plenty* [1976] 1 WLR 141).

The courts have interpreted this to include liability where the employee commits a criminal offence. In *Lister v Hesley Hall Ltd* [2001] UKHL 22, an employer was vicariously liable for the acts committed by its employee. In *Lister* the criminal act was sexual abuse and this was still sufficiently connected with his duties as an employee. Another example is *Fennelly v Connex South Eastern Ltd* [2001] IRLR 390, where a ticket inspector assaulted a commuter. The Court of Appeal held that the employer was vicariously liable because the employee was still acting within the course of his employment and had been given the power to inspect tickets. Buxton LJ held that: 'I consider it artificial to say that just because Mr Fennelly was walking on, what happened next – immediately next – was divorced from what Mr Sparrow was employed to do. The [assault] sprang directly out of the altercation' (at [18]).

RESTRICTIVE COVENANTS

Key definition: Restrictive covenants

A restrictive covenant is a restraint of trade and is intended to prevent the employee from competing with the employer once they have left their employment. Such a clause can prevent non-competition, non-poaching of colleagues and non-solicitation of clients.

An employer may wish to restrict the ability of an employee who has left their employment to work for a competitor or to set up a rival business, to poach their employees, or to solicit their customers. Including restrictive covenants in the employment contract makes commercial sense and many professionals such as accountants or lawyers will have such clauses in their contracts. There is a concern that a former employee will reveal confidential information to competitors and exploit their knowledge of the employer's customers and trade secrets. Therefore, in order to be legally enforceable, such a clause must protect a legitimate business interest (*Jack Allen (Sales and Service) Ltd v Smith* [1999] IRLR 19). However, it is important to note that such restraints must be expressly incorporated into the employment contract.

A restrictive covenant is a restraint of trade and is prima facie void (see *Nordenfelt v Maxim Nordenfelt Guns & Ammunition Co Ltd* [1894] AC 535). In order to be enforceable it must be reasonable. Therefore, when drafting such a clause it must be reasonable in terms of duration, geographical scope and nature. A restrictive covenant will only protect a legitimate business interest that requires protection. For example, using such a clause to prevent an employee from working for a rival employer in any area of their business would be unreasonable, as it would be wider than the legitimate business interest that the employer would be seeking to protect.

KEY CASE ANALYSIS: *Littlewoods Organisation Ltd v Harris*
[1977] 1 WLR 1472

Background

Harris had worked for Littlewoods, a catalogue company, and after leaving Littlewoods' employment he worked for a rival catalogue company. Littlewoods wished to prevent this and sought to rely on the restrictive covenant contained in Harris' contract.

Principle established

The Court of Appeal in *Littlewoods Organisation Ltd v Harris* [1977] 1 WLR 1472 held that a clause that prevented a former employee from working for a competitor in the United Kingdom for a year was reasonable. This was because the employer's business was a catalogue company and therefore required nationwide protection. Lord Denning MR was willing to read the original clause that had applied worldwide, to instead only apply to the United Kingdom.

In *Fitch v Dewes* [1921] 2 AC 158, a restrictive covenant that prevented a junior clerk from seeking legal employment within seven miles of the Town Hall of Tamworth, was held to be reasonable. Lord Parmoor observed that the area was not too wide:

> It is no more than adequate protection for a solicitor who desires to protect his professional secrets and to protect his clients from being enticed away by a former clerk who has had access to all his papers and has been in direct personal relation with a number of his clients. (pp. 169–170)

If a restrictive covenant is unreasonable, then the courts may apply a test known as the blue pencil test. This will involve removing the unreasonable elements and leaving the parts that are enforceable. However, the courts will not apply the blue pencil test where this will result in the contracts making a new contract. In *Francotyp-Postalia Ltd v Whitehead* [2011] EWHC 367 (Ch), the court refused to apply the blue pencil test and remove a word from the definition section of the contract to save a restrictive covenant as it would impact upon other enforceable clauses.

On-the-spot question

? Mark works for Delby Ltd as a software developer and wishes to move jobs so that he can work for a competitor. In his contract there is a restrictive covenant that states that he 'cannot work for a competitor within the first three years of leaving Delby Ltd's employment anywhere within the United Kingdom'.

Could Delby Ltd rely on the restrictive covenant to prevent Mark from working for its competitor?

Duty of mutual trust and confidence

Both the employer and employee owe each other a duty of mutual trust and confidence. This is an important duty as if it is breached then this could enable either party to terminate the employment contract.

Duty of fidelity

During the employment contract the employee owes the employer an implied duty of fidelity. This means that the employee owes a duty of good faith. The employee owes a duty of loyalty and must not compete against the employer. This means that the employee must not moonlight, that is undertake work in their own time that would compete with their employer's business. The employee must not reveal information about the employer's business and must keep all information confidential. This implied duty extends to confidentiality and to not misusing the employer's property.

Duty of confidentiality

The duty of confidentiality is implied from the relationship between the employer and employee. During the employment contract the employee must not reveal any relevant information relating to their employment and must keep all information confidential that is gained in the course of their employment. After the employment relationship is terminated the employee is still under a duty to not reveal confidential information; however, this is now a much lighter obligation and only protects information that is genuinely confidential.

KEY CASE ANALYSIS: *Faccenda Chicken Ltd v Fowler* [1986] 3 WLR 288

Background

The claimant was a business that sold chickens from refrigerated vans. It employed the defendant as its sales manager. Subsequently, the defendant used the information about sales and pricing that he had learned from the claimant in order to establish his own business.

Principle established

The Court of Appeal held that after the termination of the employment relationship, there was still a duty owed by the employee. However, the duty did not cover all confidential information, but only information that amounted to a trade secret. Therefore, the defendant was not in breach of this implied term as the information he had used was not a trade secret. Examples of what would amount to a trade secret included a chemical formula (see *Amber Size and Chemical Co Ltd v Menzel* [1913] 2 Ch 239).

The question of what amounted to a trade secret was considered in *Goldenfry Foods Ltd v Austin* [2011] EWHC 137 (QB), where it was held that there had been a breach of the duty of confidentially by former employees of the claimant. The former employees had established a rival business and had used the claimant's trade secrets.

On-the-spot question

? Mick works for Delby Ltd's engineering department and has been working on a design for a new type of door springs. His team has spent two years building and testing the new door springs. During this time Mick has met with Delby Ltd's customers and has discussed their requirements for door springs and how much they would be willing to pay. Mick retires from Delby Ltd and sets up a company manufacturing door springs. Last week he enters into a contract to supply one of Delby Ltd's largest customers with door springs.

Discuss.

WORKING TIME REGULATIONS 1998

The Working Time Regulations 1998 (WTR) protect workers and establish minimum amounts that include the entitlement to leave (reg 13), rest breaks (reg 12), the amount of daily rest that workers are entitled to (reg 10) and the maximum weekly working time (reg 4). It is possible to opt out of the WTR and certain regulations do not apply to those who can determine their own working time (reg 20).

NATIONAL MINIMUM WAGE ACT 1998

It is a criminal offence to pay a worker less than the minimum wage (s.31). The minimum wage will apply different rates depending on the age of the worker. It is increased each year. You should note that the minimum wage is not the same as the living wage, which is the amount you need in order to be able to have an adequate standard of living. In London there has been a campaign to encourage employers to pay the living wage, which is higher than the minimum wage. It should be noted that there is no legal requirement for an employer to pay the living wage; whereas, the employer must pay the minimum wage.

PARENTAL RIGHTS

Maternity and paternity leave applies to all eligible employees who qualify to have parental leave. The right to leave also extends to parents who adopt a baby. This is a complex area and we will just consider a mother who is to give birth. As an employee she will be potentially eligible, subject to the amount of time that she has worked for the employer, to take up to 52 weeks' maternity leave. During her maternity leave she will receive statutory maternity pay for the first 39 weeks, which is calculated at different amounts for the first 6 weeks and the final 33 weeks.

MOBILITY CLAUSES

Key definition: Mobility clause

A mobility clause enables the employer to ask an employee to work at another location other than the employee's contractual place of work.

The mobility clause must be expressly incorporated into the contract. The employer can only request the employee work at the locations listed in the clause. In *United Bank v Akhtar* [1989] IRLR 507, the Employment Appeal Tribunal considered the enforceability of a clause that required an employee to relocate to any part of the United Kingdom. The employee had asked for three months to arrange the move and this was refused. It was held that although the clause covered the United Kingdom, the employer was in breach of the clause, as there was an implied term that the employer should provide reasonable notice and financial assistance to enable the employee to comply with the request. The employer's behaviour had breached the implied duty of mutual trust and confidence and the employee was able to argue that he had been constructively dismissed.

BRINGING THE CONTRACT TO AN END

This next section will look at bringing the contract to an end.

Notice period

An employee who wishes to resign must give the correct contractual notice. Failure to give notice will amount to a breach of contract. We shall see below that an employer who does not give an employee the correct amount of notice before dismissing them risks facing a claim for wrongful dismissal.

Gardening leave clauses

When the employee gives notice of their intention to leave the employer's employment, or when the employer gives the employee notice that they will be dismissed, the employer in both instances may wish to remove the employee from the workplace until the employment contract has come to an end. A garden leave clause permits the employer to do this and is designed to safeguard the employer's confidential information and customer base. In *William Hill Organisation Ltd v Tucker* [1999] ICR 291, the Court of Appeal distinguished between an obligation to only pay the employee (the employee could be sent home without there being a garden leave clause), or whether there was an obligation to permit the employee to work (where there needed to be an express garden leave clause). Therefore, skilled employees who need to practise their skills on a regular basis (otherwise they would be de-skilled) will have a right to work. In *Christie v Carmichael* [2010] IRLR 1016, it was held by the Scottish Employment Appeal Tribunal that the employer of a chartered accountant did not have an obligation to provide work as the employee would not become de-skilled.

The employee must continue to receive full pay and other benefits. This would include discretionary bonuses, as in *SG v R Valuation Service Co v Boudrais* [2008] EWHC 1340 (QB), where this was a substantial part of the remuneration package. It must be remembered that a garden leave clause is a restraint of trade and is void subject to the clause being reasonable (see *Symbian Ltd v Christensen* [2001] IRLR 77). If the employee attempts to work for a competitor during the period of time covered by the garden leave clause, then the employer may apply for an injunction to prevent this.

TYPES OF DISMISSAL

There are different types of dismissal (see Figure 7.1). The employer may dismiss the employee using express words. This is known as actual dismissal. The employee may be dismissed upon the expiration of a fixed-term contract. It is also possible that the employee may claim that they have been constructively dismissed.

Constructive dismissal

This occurs where the employer commits a repudiatory breach of the employment contract. Constructive dismissal can give rise to a claim for wrongful and unfair dismissal (*Sutcliffe v Hawker Siddley Aviation Ltd* [1973] ICR 560). This could be where there has been a serious breach of health and safety or bullying by management. The repudiatory breach does not have to be the only reason why the employee resigned (see *Jones v F Sirl & Son (Furnishers) Ltd* [1997] IRLR 493). The Court of Appeal in *Meikle v Nottinghamshire* County Council [2004] ICR 1 stated that:

> The proper approach, therefore, once a repudiation of the contract by the employer has been established, is to ask whether the employee has accepted that repudiation by treating the contract of employment as at an end. It must be in response to the repudiation, but the fact that the employee also objected to the other actions or inactions of the employer, not amounting to a breach of contract, would not vitiate the acceptance of the repudiation. (at p. 11)

It is clear that the employee 'must act in sufficient time' and accept that there has been a repudiatory breach and resign (*Meikle*, at p. 16). Failure to do so will amount to the employee waiving the breach.

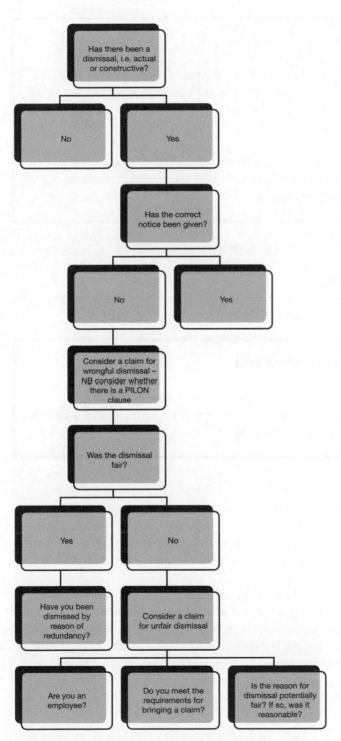

Figure 7.1 Possible claims upon dismissal

On-the-spot question

Jasmin works in one of Delby Ltd's showrooms. On Friday, while Jasmin is talking to customers, her manager, Rita, walks over and berates her for being incompetent. Jasmin is distraught as the customers and her colleagues have overheard what has been said.

Could Jasmin claim that she has been constructively dismissed? Would it matter that Jasmin has recently been looking to move jobs? Could Jasmin wait until she has found another job before accepting the breach?

WRONGFUL DISMISSAL

Key definition: Wrongful dismissal

This is a common law claim for breach of contract that a worker or an employee can bring where they have been dismissed without receiving the correct notice period, or the correct pay and other benefits due during this period.

Wrongful dismissal arises where a person has been dismissed without receiving the correct amount of notice, pay and other benefits that they should have received during the notice period. Eligibility to claim wrongful dismissal does not depend on your employment status. Therefore both an employee and a worker can bring a claim for wrongful dismissal.

Wrongful dismissal is based on there having been a breach of contract. A continuous contract of employment will last until it is terminated. In order to terminate the contract, the employer (or employee) must give the correct amount of notice. The notice requirement should be stated in the contract (i.e. the contractual notice period). Section 86(1) ERA 1996 provides a minimum statutory notice period that must be complied with. The amount of notice will depend on length of service and the maximum statutory notice period is 12 weeks. The contractual notice period may be more generous than the statutory minimum, but it must be no less.

Key definition: Fixed-term contract

A fixed-term contract will last for a predetermined amount of time. An example of someone on a fixed-term contract is a football manager, or someone who is specifically employed to cover maternity leave.

A person who is dismissed prior to the expiry of the fixed-term contract can claim wrongful dismissal. Clearly, a fixed-term contract lasting two years may risk the employer being left unable to dismiss an employee during these two years. That is why a fixed-term contract might include a break-clause. Such a clause will permit the employer to terminate the contract at an earlier date.

When does notice not have to be given?

The employer does not have to give notice where the employee, or worker, has committed a repudiatory breach of the contract. Examples include gross misconduct, theft, violence and repeatedly disobeying orders (*Boston Deep Sea Fishing and Ice Company v Ansell* (1888) 39 Ch D 339). The employee can be dismissed summarily. Where the contract has been frustrated by the employee being no longer able to perform his work, then the contract is said to have been discharged and notice does not need to be given. Examples include long-term illness and imprisonment (*FC Shepherd & Co v Jerrom* [1987] QB 301).

The employer could include a payment in lieu of notice clause in the contract (PILON). A PILON clause enables the employer to terminate the contract without giving the employee notice. It is important to note that where notice is required (even if a PILON clause has been used), the employer must give the employee the salary and benefits that the employee would have received during the notice period.

Remedies

The remedies available for wrongful dismissal are to enable the employee to recover the pay he would have received but for being prevented from serving out his notice period. The damages would include the employee's salary and other benefits.

Bringing the claim

Wrongful dismissal is essentially a claim for breach of contract and therefore can be heard by the County or High Court, or the employment tribunal. Where a claim is heard before the County or High court then there is a six-year time limit from the breach (Limitation Act 1980). The employment tribunal has a considerably shorter time limit of three months. Larger claims will be heard before the County or the High Court as there is no limit on the damages that could be recovered, whereas at the employment tribunal damages are capped at around £25,000.

UNFAIR DISMISSAL

Key definition: Unfair dismissal

Where the employer dismisses an employee for a reason that is unfair, either in terms of the circumstances or the procedure used, the employee can claim that they have been unfairly dismissed. Unfair dismissal is a statutory claim. A dismissal for certain types of reasons will be automatically unfair.

It is important to note that only employees have protection from being unfairly dismissed. The right to not be unfairly dismissed is found in s.94 ERA 1996. To claim unfair dismissal the employee must:

- have been dismissed by the employer from a fixed-term or a continuous contract of employment; or
- have been constructively dismissed as a result of the employer's conduct.

The employee must submit their claim to the employment tribunal within three months of the effective date of termination (s.97 ERA 1996). Only employees who have worked for the employer for more than two years can claim unfair dismissal (s.108 ERA 1996). However, note that for those employees dismissed for an automatically unfair reason this requirement does not apply. Certain categories of employees cannot bring a claim for unfair dismissal. These include share fishermen.

The employer has the burden to show that the dismissal was for a potentially fair reason (s.98 ERA 196). There are five potentially fair reasons: capability or qualifications, conduct, redundancy, illegality and some other substantial reason. Section 98(3) defines what is meant by capability and qualifications.

Where there has been a dismissal for an automatically unfair reason then the employer is unable to argue that it was fair to dismiss in the circumstances. The automatically unfair reasons include trade union membership, pregnancy, unfair selection for redundancy and those raising health and safety issues.

Reasonableness

The tribunal will consider whether the dismissal for a potentially fair reason was fair in both the circumstances and the procedure used. Guidance has been established by the decision of the Employment Appeal Tribunal in *Iceland Frozen Foods Ltd v Jones* [1983] ICR 16.

KEY CASE ANALYSIS: *Iceland Frozen Foods Ltd v Jones* [1983] ICR 16.

Background

An employee who had been dismissed argued that his dismissal was unfair. He had been dismissed for failing to work the security system and for deceit. The question that concerned the EAT was what the correct approach should be for determining reasonableness.

Principle established

The EAT provided guidance to determine reasonableness:

(i)   The tribunal must start by considering words of the statute.
(ii) They must consider reasonableness of the employer's conduct and not their own views.
(iii) They must not substitute their decision on the right course to adopt for that particular employer.
(iv) They must consider the 'band of reasonable responses to the employee's conduct within which one employer might reasonably take one view, another quite reasonably take another'.
(v)   As an industrial jury, they must determine whether the employer's actions fell within the band of reasonable responses.

Ensuring that the employer dismisses an employee for a valid reason is important. Even if the employee's conduct is poor, there is a risk that dismissing the employee for a minor incidence of misconduct could be held to be unfair. Employers are expected to adopt a fair procedure (*British Home Stores Ltd v Burchell* [1980] ICR 303 and *Orr v Milton Keynes Council* [2011] EWCA Civ 62) and to follow their own company disciplinary procedure or the ACAS code of practice. It must be noted that what will be reasonable will depend on the size of the employer's business as well as the circumstances of the case.

Remedies for unfair dismissal

The employment tribunal can order that the employee is reinstated (he receives his old job back) or is re-engaged (he receives a new position with the employer or an association business). This is rarely ordered, as the employment relationship will have inevitably broken down.

We will look at the types of compensation that the claimant can be rewarded:

(i) Basic award

This award is based on the number of years that the employee has worked for the employer (s.119 ERA 1996). It takes into account up to 20 years' service and for each year the employee is awarded one week's pay (capped at £450). However, note that there is a multiplier based on the age of the employee:

- for every year that the employee worked aged 41 or above he will receive one week's pay x 1.5;
- for every year that the employee worked aged 22–40 he will receive one week's pay x 1;
- for every year that the employee has worked aged 21 or under he will receive one week's pay x 0.5.

Example

For example, imagine that Rushon has worked for Delby Ltd for 30 years. His weekly pay is £670. Rushon is 49 years old.

1   We would cap Rushon's weekly pay at £450.
2   We would disregard the first 10 years of his employment at Delby Ltd.
3   We would divide the years he worked into aged 41 and over, 22–40 and 21 and under:

- 9 years aged 41 and over.
- 11 years aged 22–40.

4   We would then do the calculations:

- $9 \times £450 \times 1.5 = £4,050$
- $11 \times £450 \times 1 = £4,950$

5   The final amount would be Rushon's basic award.

It is important to note that the cap of £450 will be increased in the future and when determining the basic award you should check what the current amount is.

We will now consider how you would calculate the following claimant's basic award:

On-the-spot question

 Sonya has worked at Delby Ltd for 13 years. Sonya is 28 years old and earns £297 per week. Sonya has been unfairly dismissed and she would like to know how much her basic award would be.

(ii) Compensatory award

This award is the amount that the tribunal considers to be just and equitable in the circumstances (s.123 ERA 1996). It is based on the employee's losses post dismissal. Under s.124 ERA 1996, the maximum compensation available is £74,200. The compensation can be reduced or increased by the tribunal for a number of reasons.

REDUNDANCY

Key definition: Redundancy

This occurs where the employer has dismissed an employee for reasons including the closure of a business or the employee's particular workplace, or where there is a reduction in the need for the work that the employee performs.

Only employees are eligible to claim redundancy payments (s.135 EA 1996). According to s.139, an employee will be dismissed by way of redundancy if the dismissal is wholly or mainly attributable to the cessation of the employer's business in the place where the employee was employed, or the cessation of the employer's business for the purpose that the employee was employed for. The employee is also dismissed where the need for work of a particular kind has ceased or diminished across the business or at a particular premise. If the dismissal is not a genuine redundancy situation, then the employee will be considered to have been unfairly dismissed and eligible to claim both the basic and compensatory award.

Not only must there be a genuine redundancy, the redundancy must be both fair in the circumstances and procedure. There are different requirements for redundancies depending on the number of employees who are being made redundant (fewer than 20, 20–99 and over 100). For example, the length of consultation required for 20–99 redundancies will be 30 days before there can be a dismissal, while for 100 redundancies this is 45 days.

These requirements involve having a fair selection criteria to avoid the employer using the redundancy situation to dismiss predetermined members of staff. It will not be a redundancy if the employer could provide suitable alternative employment. However, if the employer offers the employee suitable alternative employment and the employee unreasonably refuses this, the employee will not be able to claim the statutory redundancy payment.

Redundancy award

To receive the statutory redundancy award the employee must have worked for the employer for more than two years. A claim must be made to the employment tribunal within six months of the effective date of termination. The calculation of the statutory redundancy award is the same as the basic award for unfair dismissal (see above).

CALCULATING AWARDS

You need to remember that employment law is complex and there may be many claims being brought. Therefore, you cannot simply add together the available awards for each claim and advise a client that she will receive the entire amount. The tribunal will not permit a claimant to be over compensated. It is worth remembering that the award could be reduced or increased due to a number of factors.

EQUALITY ACT 2010

For employers, the Equality Act 2010 (EA 2010) is important as it consolidates the previous legislation that had provided protection from discrimination. Employers must not discriminate against their employees and therefore it is important to understand what constitutes discrimination.

Protected characteristics

Under the EA 2010 there are nine protected characteristics (s.4). These are age, disability, gender reassignment, marriage and civil partnership, pregnancy and maternity, race, religion or belief, sex and sexual orientation. Each protected characteristic is defined by the EA 2010 and case law. We shall look at disability and religion to demonstrate how the EA 2010 operates. To look at the other protected characteristics please visit: www.legislation. gov.uk/ukpga/2010/15/contents.

Disability

Key definition: Disability

Section 6 EA 2010 defines disability as a physical or mental impairment that has a substantial and long-term adverse effect on a person's ability to carry out normal day-to-day activities.

If the employee is suffering from an addiction then this is not a mental impairment. However, in *Power v Panasonic UK Ltd* [2003] IRLR 151, it was held that if this causes a physical or mental impairment then the employee will be regarded as disabled.

Schedule 1 provides guidance on what is meant by a long-term and substantial adverse effect. A long-term effect means that the impairment should last at least 12 months, is likely to last at least 12 months or is likely to last the rest of the person's life. Substantial adverse effects relate to normal day-to-day activities and not any specialist activities (*Chief Constable of Dumfries & Galloway v Adams* [2009] ICR 1034. The employment tribunal must consider expert medical evidence (where available) when determining this point. In *Sussex Partnership NHS Foundation Trust v Norris* [2012] Eq LR 1068, the expert medical evidence did not show that the job applicant's recurring risk of infection, which was caused by suffering from immunodeficiency, had a substantial adverse impact on the applicant's ability to carry out normal day-to-day activities. However, the tribunal deduced that it would.

The focus should be on what the person cannot do, rather than what they can still do (*Goodwin v Patent Office* [1999] ICR 302). The reason for this is quite clear, as someone who is visually impaired is still capable of doing a significant number of day-to-day activities.

However, in *J v DLA Piper UK* [2010] ICR 1052, the Employment Appeal Tribunal held that in some cases it is necessary to consider what the claimant can still do:

> The ultimate question is no doubt always whether a particular capacity is substantially affected; and it is thus immaterial that other capacities may be wholly unimpaired. But in many cases, including this, considering what the claimant is still able to do, in relation to the relevant capacity, is simply a part of the exercise of assessing the extent to which that capacity is impaired. (at p. 1079)

If medical treatment is used, then the effect of the medical treatment is disregarded when determining the effect of the impairment (schedule 1, paragraph 5). Certain medical conditions are deemed to be disabilities. According to schedule 6 these are cancer, HIV infection and multiple sclerosis.

Religion or belief

Section 10 defines religion or belief. Subsection (1) states that any religion or indeed a lack of religion is protected (i.e. atheists). Subsection (2) states that any religious or philosophical belief is protected as is lack of a belief (case law on belief). From the guidance notes a philosophical belief will not automatically be protected, as the belief must meet certain conditions such as 'be a belief as to a weighty and substantial aspect of human life and behaviour' and 'not conflict with the fundamental rights of others' (this comes from the decision in *Grainger Ltd v Nicholson* [2010] 2 All ER 253).

PROHIBITED CONDUCT UNDER THE EQUALITY ACT 2010

Key definition: Prohibited conduct

The EA 2010 prohibits conduct including direct discrimination, indirect discrimination, harassment and victimisation.

The EA 2010 prohibits certain types of conduct and these apply across all the protected characteristics. However, you should note that some of these only apply to certain protected characteristics and that we will only cover a few examples of prohibited conduct. Where there has been prohibited conduct, the victim of the discrimination will be able to apply to the employment tribunal to recover damages.

Direct discrimination

> ## Key definition: Direct discrimination
>
> Section 13 prohibits direct discrimination. Direct discrimination occurs where the employer would treat an employee less favourably than she does or would treat another employee because of their protected characteristic.

There is no defence to s.13, unless the protected characteristic is age. It is not possible for the employee to argue that there had been no intention to discriminate. An example of this might be an old fashioned firm of builders that refuses to allow women to do heavy manual work on a building site, or a hospital insisting that trainee male nurses are chaperoned when working with patients (see *Moyhing v Barts & London NHS Trust* [2006] IRLR 860).

Indirect discrimination

Indirect discrimination is prohibited by s.19. This occurs where the employer applies 'a provision, criterion or practice which is discriminatory in relation to a relevant protected characteristic' of B who is their employee:

- This must be applied (or would be applied) to people who do not share B's protected characteristic.
- It must put someone sharing B's protected characteristic 'at a particular disadvantage when compared with persons with whom B does not share it' and 'it puts, or would put, B at that disadvantage when compared with persons with whom B does not share it'.

How does this work? Imagine that Francis is classified as disabled for the purposes of s.6 EA 2010. Francis's employer has a rule that all staff must work one weekend a month. Due to poor transport connections at the weekend, Francis struggles to commute to work as she cannot drive a car for medical reasons. Francis would argue that this provision would put someone who shared her protected characteristic at a particular disadvantage over her co-workers who are not disabled. Francis would argue that she is at a particular disadvantage. However, there is a defence that the employer can raise. The employer can argue that the provision, criterion or practice is a proportionate means of achieving a legitimate aim. An example of indirect discrimination is *London Underground Ltd v Edwards (No 2)* [1999] ICR 494.

KEY CASE ANALYSIS: *London Underground Ltd v Edwards (No 2)* **[1999] ICR 494**

Background

A single mother was employed as a train operator and complained that due to an introduction of a new shift pattern she would be unable to work. This was because she was now unable to arrange childcare. She was the only train operator who was unable to accept the new shift pattern.

Principle established

The relevant legislation at the time was the Sex Discrimination Act 1975, although today it would be the EA 2010. The Court of Appeal held that there had been indirect discrimination as statistically women, who were more likely to have childcare commitments than men, would find it harder to comply with the new shift pattern. The pool of comparison to determine whether discrimination had taken place was all the train operators and the Court of Appeal held that the tribunal was right to take into account their own knowledge of childcare responsibilities and the predominance of single parents who were female over single parents who were male.

Discrimination arising from disability

Section 15 EA 2010 establishes the prohibited conduct of discrimination arising from disability. This provision is different from s.13 as the employer would discriminate where he 'treats (the employee) unfavourably because of something arising in consequence of B's disability', as opposed to 'less favourably' under s.13. This gives disabled persons more protection and reverses the House of Lord's controversial decision in *Malcolm v Lewisham LBC* [2008] 1 AC 1399. The case related to a tenant of Lewisham LBC. Lord Scott discussed the example of a blind man and his dog being refused entry to a restaurant:

> The dog is not a potential beneficiary of the (disability discrimination legislation). It is the blind man who is. If he is refused entry it is not because he is blind but because he is accompanied by a dog and is not prepared to leave his dog outside. Anyone, whether sighted or blind, who was accompanied by a dog would have been treated in the *same way*. The reason for the treatment would not have related to the blindness; it would have related to the dog. (italics added, at [35])

Under s.15 there is no need to show less favourable, rather unfavourable treatment. This has increased the protection afforded to disabled persons. However, the employer would have a defence where the treatment complained of is 'a proportionate means of achieving a legitimate aim'.

Duty to make reasonable adjustments

Under s.20 there is a duty to make reasonable adjustments for disabled persons. In the employment context this would entail providing access to a building and toilet facilities, access to the kitchen and adjusting the workstation.

Harassment and victimisation

Harassment is prohibited by s.26 and could occur where the employer or a co-worker 'engages in unwanted conduct related to a relevant protected characteristic', which has the purpose (i.e. it was deliberate) or the effect of violating the employee's dignity or 'creating an intimidating, hostile, degrading, humiliating or offensive environment'. It would be possible for a heterosexual man to bring a claim if his colleagues engaged in homophobic banter at his expense, even if they knew he was heterosexual. This would be the case because the victimisation was based on his supposed sexual orientation (see *English v Thomas Sanderson Blinds Ltd* [2008] EWCA Civ 1421). Victimisation is prohibited under s.27.

Particular provisions relating to employment

Section 39 prevents discrimination for both employees and applicants. This provision is important in the employment context, especially in terms of recruitment, dismissal and opportunities such as training and promotion. Section 40 prevents the employer from harassing employees and applicants. Originally, it also used to protect employees from being harassed by a third party while in the course of their employment. This provision has been repealed.

Genuine occupational requirements

Schedule 9 lists genuine occupational requirements. Where these apply there will not be discrimination under provisions such as s.39. This protects employers who require a person of a particular gender, age or a particular religion or race for a job. For example, the Equality and Human Rights Commission has observed that: 'If a butcher has to prepare halal meat (meat that has been prepared in a way that is consistent with the Muslim faith), it might be justified to insist that this role is performed by a Muslim.'

Now that we have looked at the protected characteristics and prohibited conduct, please consider the following example:

> ## On-the-spot question
>
> **?** Karl works for Delby Ltd as a manager in its showroom. Karl's job requires him to work Monday–Friday and to be on his feet for much of the day. Unfortunately, Karl is involved in a car accident and his legs are badly injured. The doctors estimate that Karl will need to use crutches for the rest of his life. He finds it difficult to stand up for more than 15 minutes and uses medication to relieve the pain, which helps him to be on his feet for more than 30 minutes at one time. Karl has requested that he is permitted to move departments to work in the telesales team, so that he can work at a desk. Karl has also requested that he can work at home on two days a week as he finds commuting to work to be too tiring. Delby Ltd refuses to permit Karl to move departments as he does not have telesales experience, and refuses his request to work from home due to the costs in providing a laptop. In any event, the company policy prohibits all employees from working at home.
>
> Advise Karl as to whether he can claim that he has been discriminated against.

Equal pay

The EA 2010 also covers the equality of the terms offered. It prevents men and women being offered lower pay than someone of a different gender and ensures that there is equality during pregnancy and maternity leave.

HEALTH AND SAFETY

The employer owes the employee duties at common law. In *Wilsons & Clyde Coal Co Ltd v English* [1938] AC 57, the House of Lords held that:

> [T]here was a duty on the employer to take reasonable care and to use reasonable skill, first, to provide and maintain proper machinery, plant, appliances, and works; secondly, to select properly skilled persons to manage and superintend the business; and thirdly, to provide a proper system of working. (per Lord Maugham, at p. 86)

In addition to the Health and Safety at Work Act 1974 that imposes statutory duties on the employer, there are regulations that cover a variety of different health and safety issues.

SUMMARY

- It is important to determine whether someone is, or is not, an employee.
- Employees have greater statutory protection than other types of workers.
- The employee and the employer both owe each other important duties.
- If an employee is dismissed by the employer, she might be able to bring a claim for wrongful dismissal and unfair dismissal.
- The Equality Act 2010 protects individuals from being discriminated against.

FURTHER READING

Emir, A. *Selwyn's Law of Employment*, 18th edn (Oxford University Press, 2014) – a detailed and comprehensive textbook that explores the areas covered in this chapter in considerable detail.

Honeyball, S. *Honeyball and Bowers' Textbook on Employment Law*, 13th edn (Oxford University Press, 2014) – this book provides clear coverage of employment law.

Honeyball, S. *Great Debates in Employment Law* (Palgrave, 2011) – refer to this book for an informative discussion on key areas of debate in employment law.

Sargeant, M. *Discrimination and the Law* (Routledge, 2013) – this book provides detailed coverage of the Equality Act 2010.

Sargeant, M. and Lewis, D. *Employment Law*, 7th edn (Pearson, 2014) – this book offers more detail on the material covered here.

Chapter 8
Unincorporated businesses

LEARNING OBJECTIVES

After reading this chapter, you should be able to:

- understand what is meant by an unincorporated business;
- distinguish between a sole trader and a partnership;
- appreciate the rules that govern a partnership and the role of the partnership agreement;
- comprehend the potential problems that may arise when being in a partnership;
- understand how a partnership can be dissolved and the potential personal liabilities of the partners.

INTRODUCTION

In this chapter we will look at two different types of unincorporated businesses, sole traders and partnerships. We will look at why you would choose to have a business that is unincorporated, as opposed to a business that is incorporated. As you read through both this chapter and Chapter 9 you should consider those businesses that you encounter on a daily basis, and determine what type of business these are, and why might these businesses have been established in that particular way.

RUNNING A BUSINESS AS A SOLE TRADER

Key definition: Sole trader

A type of unincorporated business that is carried on by one person who is personally liable for all liabilities. There is no distinction between the sole trader and the business.

Key definition: Unincorporated business

A business that does not have a separate legal personality to that of its owners.

Where a person sets up business on their own they can choose to be a sole trader. A sole trader is a type of unincorporated business and this means that in law there is no distinction between the business owner and the business. Unlike a company, a sole trader does not have a separate legal personality and the business's assets and liabilities belong to her. If Alicia Andrews sets up a business as a sole trader and the business incurs liabilities of £500,000 and does not have any assets, then unfortunately, it will be Alicia who must pay the £500,000 from her own personal assets. This will mean that Alicia may have to sell her own assets, such as her house and car, to pay the money. If Alicia does not have the money she could be declared bankrupt. This is a significant consideration for those wishing to establish a business as a sole trader.

Lack of formalities in setting up the business

There are no formal requirements that have to be met when setting up a business as a sole trader. This is unlike an incorporated business. If you have an idea to make money you can decide to become a sole trader the moment that you read this sentence and you can cease being a sole trader as quickly as that. There are a number of points that you must consider. The first is that if there is more than one person running the business then it will be a partnership (see below). The second is that as a sole trader you will be self-employed and will have to pay income tax on any profits and pay national insurance. This will require you to contact Her Majesty's Revenue and Customs (HMRC) and to notify them of this. You will need to keep accounts and to submit the relevant information to HMRC. The third is that there are restrictions on what you can call your business, as you must not use a name that implies that you are running an incorporated business. You can either use your own name, or have a business name, but in any event you must state on all correspondence and at your premises that you are trading under the business name. So for Alicia this would be 'Alicia Andrews t/a Learn French Quickly'. The relevant rules for the information that a sole trader must disclose to the public and the restrictions on the business's name are contained in the Companies Act 2006 (CA 2006).

Lack of formalities when running the business

Unlike a company, there are no formalities required when running a business as a sole trader. The financial affairs of the business are not made public.

RUNNING A BUSINESS AS AN ORDINARY PARTNERSHIP

Key definition: Partnership

This is a type of unincorporated business and is created where two or more persons carry on a business together with the intention of making a profit.

In this section of the chapter we will consider ordinary partnerships. Imagine that Noor, Philippe, Sandra and Joshua wish to go into business together. As there is more than one of them they would not be able to be a sole trader, unless the other three are content to just be employees. The four of them could go into business together as a partnership. The type of partnership that we will be exploring is an ordinary partnership and is governed by the Partnership Act 1890.

Why might you set up a partnership?

An ordinary partnership is an unincorporated business and does not have a separate legal personality and therefore there is no legal distinction between the partnership and the partners. This is significant as in the event that the partnership cannot afford to pay its liabilities it will be the partners who will be personally liable for all outstanding liabilities. We shall see that the partners need to be aware from the outset that the other partners' actions could result in all the partners being liable. Therefore, Noor, Philippe, Sandra and Joshua will need to be able to trust each other. This is different than being a sole trader, where you make all the decisions and are responsible for any liabilities incurred.

Partnership Act 1890

If Noor, Philippe, Sandra and Joshua wish to form a partnership then they should make sure that they understand the Partnership Act 1890 (PA 1890). It is not a particularly lengthy Act and its provisions are relatively clear. The PA 1890 provides mandatory rules that will apply to all partnerships, and fall-back provisions which the parties are able to change in accordance with their own agreement. The PA 1890 can best be described as the rulebook and a failure to understand how its terms will affect the partnership could be detrimental to the partners. This is why a lawyer should advise the parties when they decide to form a partnership.

Setting up a partnership

Noor, Philippe, Sandra and Joshua wish to form a partnership. We shall see how they would go about doing this.

The partnership must comply with the statutory definition

Section 1(1) of the PA 1890 states that '[p]artnership is the relation which subsists between persons carrying on a business in common with a view of profit'. This means that there must be two or more persons and this is a condition that Noor, Philippe, Sandra and Joshua clearly satisfy. Additionally, as they will be working together and intend to make a profit, Noor, Philippe, Sandra and Joshua would meet the statutory definition of a partnership. The consequences of being in a partnership are illustrated by the decision in *Hodson v Hodson* [2009] EWCA Civ 1042.

KEY CASE ANALYSIS: *Hodson v Hodson* [2009] EWCA Civ 1042

Background

In *Hodson v Hodson* [2009] EWCA Civ 1042, the issue was whether the appellant was in a partnership with another defendant. The appellant argued that there was no partnership as she had sold 99 per cent of the legal practice and had only retained the additional 1 per cent so that she could supervise the new owner, as the Law Society had mandated a supervision requirement.

Principle established

The Court of Appeal held that the appellant and the new owner were in a partnership as the partnership deed met the requirements of s.1(1) PA 1890. Importantly, the legal practice would not have been in business without the appellant's supervisory capacity. The decision meant that the appellant was liable for damages awarded by a court against the partnership.

So long as the requirements in s.1(1) PA 1890 are met there will be a partnership even if one of the partners does not receive a share of the profits. This was the case in *M Young Legal Associates Ltd v Zahid (A Firm)* [2006] EWCA Civ 613 where a partner was just paid a salary. The court held that there was a partnership in order for the partners to practice together as solicitors. It was held that a partner regardless of whether he receives a share of the profits, or just a salary, would still be jointly liable for the partnership's liabilities.

When is a partnership created?

In law a partnership is created as soon as the statutory requirement in s.1(1) is met. This point is demonstrated in the House of Lords' decision in *Khan v Miah* [2000] 1 WLR 2123.

KEY CASE ANALYSIS: *Khan v Miah* [2000] 1 WLR 2123

Background

The claimant and defendant had decided to go into business together as proprietors of a restaurant. They had acquired a suitable premise and had fitted it out as a restaurant. However, the relationship had broken down and prior to the restaurant opening the claimant had decided to end the joint venture. The question was whether there was a partnership. The Court of Appeal had held that there was no partnership as the business had yet to trade.

Principle established

The House of Lords held that the Court of Appeal was wrong to hold that there could be no partnership prior to the business trading. Lord Millett (at p. 2127) was critical of the narrow approach taken by the Court of Appeal:

> [The Court of Appeal] described the business which the parties agreed to carry on together as the business of a restaurant, meaning the preparation and serving of meals to customers, and asked themselves whether the restaurant had commenced trading by the relevant date. But this was an impossibly narrow view of the enterprise on which the parties agreed to embark. They did not intend to become partners in an existing business. They did not agree merely to take over and run a restaurant. They agreed to find suitable premises, fit them out as a restaurant and run the restaurant once they had set it up. The acquisition, conversion and fitting out of the premises and the purchase of furniture and equipment were all part of the joint venture, were undertaken with a view of ultimate profit, and formed part of the business which the parties agreed to carry on in partnership together.

> There is no rule of law that the parties to a joint venture do not become partners until actual trading commences. The rule is that persons who agree to carry on a business activity as a joint venture do not become partners until they actually embark on the activity in question. It is necessary to identify the venture in order to decide whether the parties

> have actually embarked upon it, but it is not necessary to attach any particular name to it. Any commercial activity which is capable of being carried on by an individual is capable of being carried on in partnership.
>
> It is clear that Lord Millett viewed the preparatory steps carried out by the parties as being very important and sufficient to give rise to a partnership as they were being undertaken with a view to make a profit. We can see that such an approach is sensible as a business does not start the moment the first paying customers come through the door, but rather when you lay the groundwork in order to establish the business. His Lordship observed that:
>
> > The work of finding, acquiring and fitting out a shop or restaurant begins long before the premises are open for business and the first customers walk through the door. Such work is undertaken with a view of profit, and may be undertaken as well by partners as by a sole trader.
>
> The consequences of this decision is that a partnership was held to exist and therefore the obligations, duties and rules about property owner and profits are applicable even before the business commences trading.

The rules for determining existence of a partnership are listed in s.2 PA 1890. Section 2(3) concerns the effect of an individual receiving a share of the partnership's profits; it states that receiving 'a share of the profits of a business is prima facie evidence that he is a partner in the business'. Therefore, a person who receives a share of the profits would need to bring evidence to rebut this presumption. Subsection (3) must be read with paragraphs (a)–(e) which list circumstances where receiving a share of profits does not make a person a partner.

The firm

Key definition: Firm

This term refers to the persons who have entered into a partnership and they are referred to collectively as the firm.

Under the PA 1890 the word firm is used to refer to a partnership. Section 4 states that, '[p]ersons who have entered into partnership with one another are for the purposes of this Act called collectively a firm, and the name under which their business is carried on is called the firm-name'. This is why legal practices are referred to as firms, as they have been set up as partnerships.

The partnership agreement

There is no requirement that Noor, Philippe, Sandra and Joshua are required to draft a written partnership agreement. As soon as the requirements in s.1(1) are satisfied they will be regarded in law as a partnership. If they do not agree specific terms as to how the partnership will be governed, then the PA 1890 will apply and provide a set of rules to determine how the partnership will be run. Noor, Philippe, Sandra and Joshua could have agreed certain terms such as payment of a salary and the sharing of profit orally and this would still be effective. However, in the interests of certainty and ensuring that the partnership agreement reflects Noor, Philippe, Sandra and Joshua's true intentions it is advisable that there is a written partnership agreement. The written partnership agreement does not have to be executed by deed. You will see that many of the fall-back rules provided by the PA 1890 may not suit every partnership and so it is important that the partnership agreement is clear as to what will happen with regards to the sharing of the profits and other important considerations.

The partnership agreement can be varied at a later date by the consent of all the partners. The partner's consent can either be express or inferred from a course of dealings between the partners (s.19 PA 1890).

In the partnership agreement it is possible to create a fixed-term partnership, a partnership for a specific task, or a partnership at will. It is important that Noor, Philippe, Sandra and Joshua consider how long they wish to be in business together.

No need to register a partnership at Companies House

In Chapter 9 we shall see that in order to create an incorporated business such as a limited liability partnership or a private company limited by shares there are requirements that need to be satisfied before the business can be registered. These requirements relate to the documentation and fee that are stipulated by the legislation governing each type of business and these must be submitted to Companies House. The advantage of setting up a partnership is that none of these requirements apply. Equally, none of the ongoing reporting requirements apply to partnerships and the partnership's affairs are not made public on the register at Companies House. This is important as incorporated businesses must submit their accounts to Companies House and anyone is able to view the business's financial health.

Naming restrictions

The Companies Act 2006 (CA 2006) contains restrictions on what the partnership can be called. The restrictions do not prevent 'individuals carrying on business in partnership under a name consisting of the surnames of all the partners without any addition other than a permitted addition' (s.1192(2(b)). So if Julia Smith and Richard Wells were to go into partnership it could be called 'Smith and Wells'. However, they could use permitted additions – their forenames 'Julia Smith and Richard Wells' or their initials 'J. Smith and R. Wells' (s.1192(3)(b)). Section 1197 states that it is an offence to have a company that is misleading as to the type of business that it is. Therefore, the partnership could not be 'Julia Smith and Richard Wells Ltd', as this would suggest that the partnership is a private limited company. A partnership could trade under a business name and not be called by its partners' surnames. However, it is also important to note the extensive restrictions on the choice of business names under the CA 2006. Unsurprisingly, when naming a partnership it is important to avoid incurring liability under the tort of passing off. We explored this tort in Chapter 4 and there will be liability where a name is similar to that of another business and this causes confusion for customers or takes customers away from the other business due to the similarity of the name (see *Ewing v Buttercup Margarine Co Ltd* [1917] 2 Ch 1).

Disclosure of important information

A partnership must state the name of each member of the partnership and the place of business on all business letters and other important correspondence (s.1202(1) CA 2006). For the purposes of s.1202(1)), if there are more than 20 partners you only need to disclose the names of the first 20 (s.1203(1)). However, a full list must be kept at the partnership's place of business and anyone is able to inspect this list (s.1203(2) and (3)). The disclosure requirements must also be displayed in a prominent position at the partnership's premises or any other place where customers or suppliers have access (s.1204(1)).

On-the-spot question

? Noor, Philippe, Sandra and Joshua decide to set up a partnership. They decide that the written partnership agreement will be signed on 1 August and on this date they will officially become partners of the firm. In the meantime they all meet up at Joshua's flat and think of ways to make money. They decide that Sandra will not receive any share of the profits, but will instead receive a salary of £17,000 a year. On 18 July, Philippe is sent by the others to purchase £40,000 worth of stock from ABC Ltd and plans to use this for the partnership.

Consider the following points:

- On 18 July was the partnership in existence? Or did the partnership only come into existence on 1 August?
- Would Sandra be regarded as a partner if she did not receive a share of the profits?
- What could the partnership be called and what information would need to be disclosed and how would this disclosure be achieved?

Running the partnership

All the partners are entitled to take part in the management of the partnership (s.24(5) PA 1890). The partners could decide expressly or impliedly that the management could be restricted to certain partners. If the partners are in dispute about 'ordinary matters connected with the partnership', then s.24(8) states that a majority of the partners may take the decisions. There is a restriction here as 'no change may be made in the nature of the partnership business without the consent of all existing partners'. This means that decisions reflecting the nature of the partnership cannot just be taken by a majority of the partners. Section 24(8) can be amended by the partner's express or implied agreement.

No entitlement to a salary

In Noor, Philippe, Sandra and Joshua's partnership none of the partners are entitled to be paid a salary (s.24(6)). However, the partners could have agreed expressly or impliedly to change this. A salary could be paid, for example, if Noor is devoting more time than any of the other partners to carrying out the partnership's business. In that case the partnership could decide to pay her a salary.

Equal division of profits (and losses)

When the partnership is created Noor, Philippe, Sandra and Joshua will subscribe by allocating capital to the partnership. If they all intend to contribute an equal amount and devote roughly the same amount of time working then equal division of profits would make sense. Section 24(1) PA 1890 states that '[a]ll the partners are entitled to share equally in the capital and profits of the business, and must contribute equally towards the losses whether of capital or otherwise sustained by the firm'. The partners can change this through express or implied agreement and could agree that there will be an unequal division of profits and losses.

Partnership property

The partnership does not have a separate legal personality and therefore it cannot hold property in its own right and so the property is owned by the partners. This means that any property held and applied by the partners for the purposes of the partnership must not be used for any other purpose (s.20(1) PA 1890). We can see how this applies in practice when we consider the Court of Appeal's decision in *Popat v Shonchhatra* [1997] 1 WLR 1367.

KEY CASE ANALYSIS: *Popat v Shonchhatra* [1997] 1 WLR 1367

Background

In *Popat v Shonchhatra* a partnership had been entered into and the leasehold of a shop acquired by the partners as joint tenants. Popat left the partnership and Shonchhatra purchased the freehold of the shop. Later on Shonchhatra sold the freehold and the goodwill of the business.

Principle established

The Court of Appeal held that as soon as any asset was contributed to the partnership it became partnership property and no one partner could argue that he owned a specific asset. The partners both had a propriety interest in all the assets. The freehold had been purchased with partnership assets and therefore Popat was entitled to a share of the sale price.

Section 21 PA 1890 states that anything purchased with partnership property is considered to belong to the firm. In *Nadeem v Rafiq* [2007] EWHC 2959 (Ch), the issue involved whether there was a partnership and if there was whether the premise that had been purchased was partnership property. The court answered both issues in the affirmative. Both partners had contributed to the deposit to purchase the premises through the business bank account. Therefore, the premises was an asset of the partnership.

The ability of a partner to bind the partnership

In this next section we shall see the problems that may arise for Noor, Philippe, Sandra and Joshua as partners. We will look at the authority of each partner to bind the partnership, which really means incurring liability for all the partners (see Figure 8.1).

Section 5 PA 1890 states that:

- Every partner is an agent of the firm and his other partners for the purpose of the business of the partnership
- and the acts of every partner who does any act for carrying on in the usual way business of the kind carried on by the firm of which he is a member binds the firm and his partners

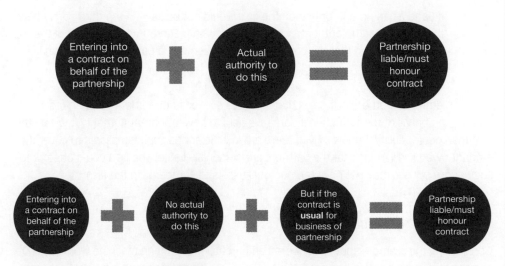

Figure 8.1 In what circumstances under s.5 PA 1890 can an individual partner bind the partnership?

- unless the partner so acting has in fact no authority to act for the firm in the particular matter, and the person with whom he is dealing either knows that he has no authority
- or does not know or believe him to be a partner.

This is an important section and it is necessary to consider each line to see how it applies in practice. We will now apply s.5 to Noor, Philippe, Sandra and Joshua's partnership (the firm):

- Sandra is an agent of the firm and the other partners and the firm does not have a distinct legal personality. As an agent of the firm Sandra can enter into contracts on behalf of the firm, although this must be for the purpose of the partnership's business.
- If Sandra enters into a contract with a third party on behalf of the firm then the firm will be liable to honour that contract and will be liable for any debts incurred.
- This makes sense if the other partners have agreed for Sandra to enter into that particular contract or contracts of this type, as then Sandra will have actual authority.
- However, what if Sandra was told that she cannot enter into a contract as all the partners must approve this type of decision? In that case the firm will be liable for the contract if Sandra's act was for the 'carrying on in the usual way business of the kind carried on by the firm'. The firm would have to honour the contract if it was a contract that a partner for that type of firm would usually enter into. This is apparent authority and will bind the firm in the absence of Sandra having actual authority.

- If Sandra had no authority then the firm would not be liable if the third party knew that Sandra had no authority, or did not know that Sandra was a partner of the firm and believed that the contract was between it and Sandra in her personal capacity.

The problem for the other partners is that if Sandra exceeds her authority and enters into a contract on behalf of the firm, then if Sandra is held to have apparent authority it will be the firm that incurs liability. Importantly, if there are insufficient partnership assets to cover the amount owed it will mean that the partners are personally liable. The firm could attempt to sue Sandra but she may not have the personal assets to compensate the firm.

When will the firm by bound?

Considering the example above, if Sandra had purchased a printing machine worth £4,000 and the firm was a printing business, then it is likely that the firm would be bound. However, there will be times when the contract entered into by a partner will be held not to be usual for a particular partnership's business.

I) PREPOSTEROUS INVESTMENT SCHEME

In *JJ Coughlan Ltd v Ruparelia* [2003] EWCA Civ 1057, a firm of solicitors was held not to be bound by a partner's statements, as the transaction and the partner's preposterous promises as to the expected risk free returns were not something that was within the ordinary course of business of a solicitor. The partner had promised the claimant a risk free investment scheme. Once the money was invested, the partner would manage the scheme. However, the scheme was fraudulent and the partner was held personally liable for deceit.

II) LIABILITY FOR FRAUD WHERE AN UNDERTAKING IS MADE WITHIN THE USUAL COURSE OF BUSINESS

KEY CASE ANALYSIS: *United Bank of Kuwait v Hammoud* [1988] 1 WLR 1051

Background

Mr Emmanuel, a partner in a firm of solicitors, had made an undertaking to a number of banks that turned out to be fraudulent. The question was whether the firm was liable for the undertaking given by a partner.

Principle established

The Court of Appeal held that as the banks when they relied on the undertaking would have seen this as something given in the usual course of a solicitor's business, then the firm was liable. Lord Donaldson MR explained why the firm was liable:

> The banks, knowing that Mr. Emmanuel was a practising solicitor with established firms, were entitled to assume the truth of what he stated unless alerted to the fact that the contrary might be the case. There was nothing to alert them. All that could be said was that they ought to have known that their knowledge was incomplete but there was nothing known to them which was wholly inconsistent with the facts as they were asserted by Mr. Emmanuel. (at p. 1066)

The partners might agree to restrict the ability of a partner to bind the firm. If a partner breaches this agreement then he will be liable to the other partners. The agreement will only be binding on third parties who are aware of the restriction (s.8 PA 1890).

Liability of the individual partners

All partners are bound by acts done on behalf of the firm (s.6 PA 1890). This could be where a contract has been entered into or a guarantee has been given. Looking at s.5 above we can see that even where one partner acts without the authority of the other partners and incurs a liability, then the other partners could be personally liable if the partnership has insufficient assets. Section 9 states that '[e]very partner in a firm is liable jointly with the other partners . . . for all debts and obligations of the firm incurred while he is a partner . . .'. This means that if the business owes £100,000 to its creditors and only has £10,000 in assets, the creditors can sue the partners in their personal capacity as they all will be jointly liable for the debt. If Philippe, Sandra and Joshua have no assets and declare bankruptcy, then it will be Noor who will end up paying off the business's debts. While the firm will be liable for any tort committed by a partner where he or she acts with actual authority or within 'the ordinary course of the business of the firm', the individual partners will also be jointly and severally liable (ss.10 and 12).

A liability of a non-partner

It is not only actual partners who will incur liability. A non-partner who holds herself out, or allows another to hold her out as a partner, will be liable where a third party has on the basis of this 'representation given credit to the firm' (s.14(1)). This makes sense as in the event that the firm does not pay the third party for the goods, the third party has been led to believe that he can recover the money from the alleged partner and it would be unfair if that was not the case.

On-the-spot question

? Noor, Philippe, Sandra and Joshua are in a partnership that provides catering for events. They have agreed that all the partners must approve any contract over £1,000. On Monday, Joshua walks past Mega Kitchen Ltd's showroom and sees an industrial oven on sale for £13,000. This particular oven runs on solar power and can be used anywhere. The showroom manager explains to Joshua that the oven usually costs £18,000 and that if you buy four ovens you will receive a further discount of 10 per cent. Joshua thinks that the deal is too good to be true and enters into a contract to purchase four ovens at £46,800. The money is due in 14 days' time. On Wednesday the invoice arrives at the firm's offices and the other partners are shocked to see what Joshua has done. Sandra telephones Mega Kitchens Ltd to explain; however, she is informed that a contract is a contract and that the money is owed. Philippe logs into the firm's online bank account and sees that the firm has only £3,000. This is in addition to its assets which are worth £4,000. A quick look on an online auction site reveals that the ovens are worth £2,000 each secondhand.

Noor, Philippe and Sandra are concerned that the firm may have to pay for the ovens and that there are not enough assets to cover the money due. They are aware that Joshua lives with his parents and has £500 in savings.

Advise Noor, Philippe and Sandra about their potential liabilities with respect to the money owed to Mega Kitchens Ltd.

Right to be indemnified and money lent to the firm

Imagine that Philippe has spent his own money to pay for goods to be used by the partnership. Philippe will want to be indemnified by the firm for the money that he has spent. Section 24(2) permits a partner to be indemnified where the payment that he has made or the liability that he has incurred was in 'the ordinary and proper conduct of the business of the firm' or was made in order to save or preserve the firm's property. When the partnership is formed the partners will each subscribe capital, which will be used to acquire premises and stock. However, it may be necessary for a partner to loan additional money to the partnership and on this money she will be entitled to be paid 5 per cent interest (s.24(3)). These rights can be excluded by the express or implied agreement of the partners.

Bookkeeping

The partnership's books need to be kept at the firm's place of business and each partner should be able to inspect the accounts (s.24(9)).

Duties of the partners

The partners are fiduciaries and owe fiduciary duties to each other. According to Lord Eldon LC in *Const v Harris* (1824) Turn & R 495, at 525 they are expected 'to be true and faithful to each other'. These rules were developed in equity and are extremely strict. In Chapter 6 we looked at the definition of a fiduciary when we explored the duties of an agent to his principal. The PA 1890 contains a number of statutory duties.

According to s.28 PA 1890, '[p]artners are bound to render true accounts and full information of all things affecting the partnership to any partner or his legal representatives'. This means that the partners cannot hide information and must make a full disclosure about all monies made from business transactions. Partners cannot without the consent of the other partners make private profits 'from any transaction concerning the partnership, or from any use by him of the partnership property name or business connexion' (s.29(1)). This means that if Noor uses a van that had been purchased with the firm's money for her gardening business at weekends, then she would be in breach of s.29(1) as she is using the partnership's property and should account for the use of the van.

Finally, s.30 prevents a partner from competing against the firm. This section will be breached where a partner 'carries on any business of the same nature as and competing with that of the firm' and the consequences of this will be that the partner must give the firm all the profit that he has made. An example of how these duties can be breached is *Broadhurst v Broadhurst* [2006] EWHC 2727 (Ch). In this case the partnership involved the importation and sale of cars. It was alleged by one partner that the other had breached his duties. There were a number of alleged breaches which the court accepted including lending a car that the partnership owed to a third party, which had caused the car to deteriorate and decrease in value, and lying about the fact that a car had been sold and thereby not disclosing the sale of an expensive car to his wife by pretending that the car was still for sale.

Leaving the partnership

A partner may decide that they wish to retire from the partnership. Simply by deciding to retire from the partnership will not mean that the partner avoids liability for any outstanding debts that existed prior to his retirement (s.17(2)). Section 17(3) provides for the outgoing partner to enter into an agreement with the remaining partners of the newly constituted firm (i.e. without the old partners) and the creditors to discharge all liabilities. It is possible for the outgoing partner to be liable to future creditors of the firm if they believed that he is still a partner. Section 36 states that the outgoing partner must take steps to give notice of the change and in England or Wales he would do this by taking out an advertisement in the *London Gazette*.

Expelling a partner

Section 25 PA 1890 states that '[n]o majority of the partners can expel any partner unless a power to do so has been conferred by express agreement between the partners'. So if Noor, Philippe and Sandra decide that they could no longer work with Joshua and wish to expel him from the partnership then they could not do this unless the partnership agreement permitted expulsion. In this case they will need to dissolve the partnership (see below).

New partners

No new partners may join the partnership unless all the existing partners consent to this (s.24(7)). This is the general rule and can be modified by the partners' express or implied agreement.

Dissolution/Terminating the partnership

If a partnership is not for a fixed term then it will be a partnership at will. A partner could decide to determine the partnership and dissolve it by giving notice to the other partners (s.26(1)). A partnership will also dissolve if it was established for a specific adventure and that adventure has been completed (s.32). The partnership will also be dissolved if a partner dies or is declared bankrupt (s.33(1)). The partnership will be dissolved if it becomes unlawful for the firm to continue (s.34).

Under section 35 the partners can ask the court to dissolve a partnership. This will occur where the consent of all partners cannot be obtained. The partnership will be dissolved for reasons including where a partner 'is guilty of conduct that is calculated to prejudicially affect the carrying on of the business', or where a partner

> fully or persistently commits a breach of the partnership agreement, or otherwise so conducts himself in matters relating to the partnership business that it is not reasonably practicable for the other partner or partners to carry on the business in partnership with him.

WHAT HAPPENS TO FINAL ASSETS WHEN THE PARTNERSHIP IS DISSOLVED?

Section 44 provides how the final assets will be dealt with if the partnership is dissolved (Figure 8.2).

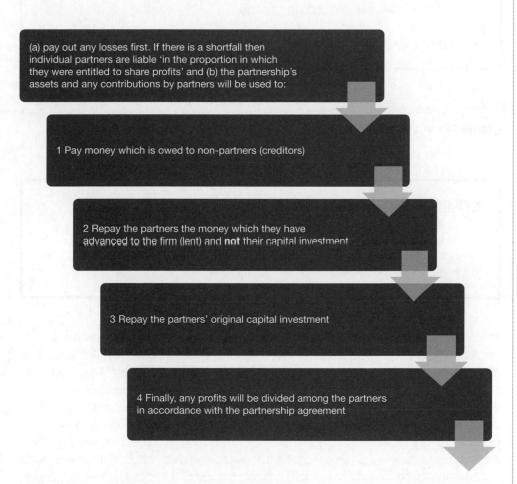

(a) pay out any losses first. If there is a shortfall then individual partners are liable 'in the proportion in which they were entitled to share profits' and (b) the partnership's assets and any contributions by partners will be used to:

1 Pay money which is owed to non-partners (creditors)

2 Repay the partners the money which they have advanced to the firm (lent) and **not** their capital investment

3 Repay the partners' original capital investment

4 Finally, any profits will be divided among the partners in accordance with the partnership agreement

Figure 8.2 Section 44 PA 1890 governs what happens when a partnership is dissolved

On-the-spot question

? Noor, Philippe, Sandra and Joshua decide to dissolve the partnership. They each subscribed £3,000 capital to the partnership and subsequently Sandra lent the partnership £5,000. The partnership has the following assets, £5,000 in the bank account and stock in Noor's garage that could be resold for around £6,000. There is also £5,700 which is owed to various creditors.

How would s.44 PA 1890 apply here?

LIMITED PARTNERSHIPS

Key definition: Limited partnership

A type of partnership where there is a distinction between the general members who have unlimited liability for the firm's debts and limited partners whose liability is limited to the extent of their capital contribution to the firm.

The Limited Partnership Act 1907 (LPA 1907) created a new type of partnership where a partnership could have two types of members, general partners who would be liable for all the firm's liabilities and limited partners, who will only be liable to the extent of their capital or property contribution to the partnership (s.4(1)). The Partnership Act 1890 applies to this type of partnership, unless it is inconsistent with the LPA 1907 (s.7). A limited partner is not allowed to take part in the management of the firm and neither does he have the power to bind the firm (s.6(1)). There is a duty to register the limited partnership at Companies House and this must include the proscribed details that must be supplied, including the names of the limited partners and the amount that they have contributed to the limited partnership (ss.8 and 8A). The name of the limited partnership must end with 'limited partnership' or 'LP' (s.8B).

SUMMARY

- A sole trader is a type of unincorporated business that does not have a separate legal personality.

- A partnership is an unincorporated business and does not have a separate legal personality.
- A partnership is governed by a partnership agreement or in the absence of any agreed terms by the Partnership Act 1890.

FURTHER READING

MacIntyre, E. *Business Law*, 6th edn (Pearson, 2013) – this textbook provides additional detail on the material covered in this chapter.

Marson, J. *Business Law*, 3rd edn (Oxford University Press, 2013) – you should refer to this textbook for additional detail on partnerships and sole traders.

Morse, G. *Partnership Law*, 7th edn (Oxford University Press, 2010) – this is an extremely detailed and well-written text that explores partnership law.

Chapter 9
Incorporated businesses

LEARNING OBJECTIVES

After reading this chapter, you should be able to:

- understand the distinction between incorporated and unincorporated businesses;
- appreciate why an ordinary partnership may wish to become a limited liability partnership;
- distinguish between public limited companies and private limited companies;
- comprehend the significance of the veil of incorporation and in what circumstances will the courts pierce the veil;
- understand the extent of the duties owed by a director and the rights that the shareholders have.

INTRODUCTION

This chapter considers the different types of incorporated business structures that you will encounter as part of your studies (Figure 9.1). Each of the different business structures covered in this chapter has a separate legal personality to that of its owners. This means that in law the business, because it has been incorporated at Companies House, is distinct

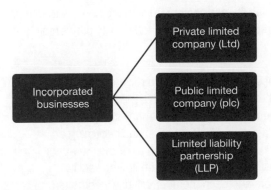

Figure 9.1 Chapter overview

from whoever may own it. The separation between the business and its owners is significant and it offers protection to those who want to protect their personal assets in the event that the business becomes insolvent. In this chapter we will look at limited liability partnerships, public limited companies and private limited companies. As you work through this chapter it is useful to consider why people in business choose to set up each of the three different types of incorporated businesses.

LIMITED LIABILITY PARTNERSHIP ACT 2000

In Chapter 8 we explored unincorporated businesses that included ordinary partnerships, which as you will remember did not have a separate legal personality. For example, if Ed, David and Nick decide to set up a partnership then the liabilities of the partnership will be indistinct from all three of the partners. So, if the partnership accrued £500,000 in liabilities to its creditors, then all three of the partners would be liable to repay this, even if it meant that they had to sell their own personal assets to do this. This type of partnership is regulated by the Partnership Act 1890 and there is a risk that partners will have unlimited liability for the debts of the partnership. The Limited Liability Partnership Act 2000 (LLPA 2000) has provided that those businesses that wish to operate as a partnership can enjoy limited liability without having to become a company. A limited liability partnership has a separate legal personality to its members (s.1(2)). In order to incorporate a limited liability partnership the requirements in s.2 must be met. Section 2(1) requires that 'two or more persons associated for carrying on a lawful business with a view to profit must have subscribed their names to an incorporation document'. The content of the incorporation document is laid out in subsection (2). The members of the limited liability partnership are not employees (s.4(4)). The members' relationship with each other is governed by the partnership agreement (s.5). The schedule to the LLPA 2000 states that the name of a limited liability partnership must end with limited liability partnership or llp or LLP. You will typically see that many law firms and accountancy firms have chosen to become limited liability partnerships. However, it should be noted that there are considerably more administrative requirements with a limited liability partnership than an ordinary partnership. The registration and continual notification requirements for a limited liability partnership are not that dissimilar to that of a company.

There are differences between a limited liability partnership and a private company limited by shares. In a company it will be the directors, who may or may not be shareholders, who will conduct the management of its affairs. In many companies there is no correlation between being a shareholder (one of the owners) and becoming a director of the company. Whereas, in a limited liability partnership all of the members will take part in the management of the business. The profits of the limited liability partnerships are shared among the members and each member will pay income tax on his share of the profit.

THE COMPANIES ACT 2006

The Companies Act 2006 (CA 2006) is 1,297 sections in length and was the product of a comprehensive reform of company law. The CA 2006 replaced the Companies Act 1985.

TYPES OF COMPANIES

In this chapter we will explore limited companies. A limited company is one where the liability of its members is limited by shares or by guarantee. However, a company can be unlimited and this will mean that the liability of its members is unlimited (s.3 CA 2006).

Public limited companies

Members of a public company can have their liability limited by shares or by guarantee. A public company will be listed on the stock exchange and any member of the public is able to purchase shares in the company and to sell their own shares. It is possible for a company to be incorporated as a public company and then to become private (ss.97–101). Equally, the opposite can happen (ss.90–96). This would happen if ABC Ltd wanted to raise money to compete against its international competitors. If it was a public company then it could raise additional funds by issuing shares on the stock exchange.

Private limited companies

A private limited company could be incorporated and have its members' liability limited by shares. This would mean that in the event that the company became insolvent the shareholders would only be liable up to the extent of their shareholding. Alternatively, the company could be incorporated and have its members' liability limited by guarantee. This would mean that in the event that the company becomes insolvent the members would guarantee to pay a specific amount.

SETTING UP A COMPANY

In this chapter we will look at a private company that has been limited by shares. This type of company is the most common type of incorporated business that is used in the United Kingdom. We shall see the reasons for this below. In order to set up a company, a number of important steps need to be completed. It is important to remember that a company will not exist until Companies House issues a certificate of incorporation.

Promoters

> ### Key definition: Promoter
>
> A person who undertakes to establish a company and takes the steps that are necessary in order to achieve this.
>
> ### Key definition: Pre-incorporation contract
>
> A contract entered into by the promoters prior to the incorporation of the company. The promoters will be personally liable on a pre-incorporation contract.

Imagine that Karl and Tom are partners in a business that renovates old sport cars. They decide in order to develop their business that they will form a private company limited by shares. Here Karl and Tom would be known as the promoters of the yet to exist company and they would be the individuals who would take all the necessary steps to set up the company. Lord Cockburn CJ in *Twycross v Grant* (1877) 2 CPD 469 observed that '[a] promoter, I apprehend, is one who undertakes to form a company with reference to a given project and to set it going, and who takes the necessary steps to accomplish that purpose' (at p. 541). Once the formation of the company is completed, an individual is no longer regarded as a promoter.

Promoters are fiduciaries who owe special duties to the yet to be incorporated company. In their capacity as promoters Karl and Tom would need to be careful, as promoters will be personally liable for any contracts that they have entered into, even if these contracts are purportedly made on behalf of the company. This is because the company does not yet exist and even when the company comes into existence they will still be liable on any contracts that they entered into before the issuing of the certificate of incorporation. In Chapter 6 we saw that agents may have any contracts that they entered into without authorisation ratified by their principals. However, this does not apply to promoters who cannot at a later date ask the company (i.e. the decision will be taken by Karl and Tom in their new capacity as directors) to ratify the contract. This is because, according to the decision *Kelner v Baxter* (1866–67) LR 2 CP 174, in order to ratify a contract a principal must be in existence at the time when the contract was made. Clearly, with a pre-incorporation contract made by the promoters this is not the case, as the company was not in existence at the time.

Worked example

Imagine that Karl and Tom decide to establish a company on Thursday. However, on Tuesday they enter into a contract with Adam to lease his barn for ten years. The company is subsequently incorporated and two years later the company starts to lose money and is unable to pay its many creditors. The company is declared insolvent. We have seen in Chapter 8 that the big disadvantage of being an unincorporated business is that you are personally liable for the business's losses. While Karl and Tom would not be liable for any debts incurred post incorporation, they would still be liable on the pre-incorporation contract they entered into with Adam. Applying the decision in *Kelner v Baxter*, they could not argue that the company had ratified the contract and therefore the company and not themselves personally would be liable. However, the company could have entered into a contract of novation with Adam. This means that the company contracts on the same terms as the original pre-incorporation contract and this releases the promoters from personal liability (*Natal Land and Colonization Company Ltd v Pauline Colliery and Development Syndicate Ltd* [1904] AC 120). We have seen that Adam can sue the promoters for a breach of the pre-incorporation contract, and if Adam is in breach of his obligations then the promoters may sue him.

Off-the-shelf company

Before we look at the steps needed to establish a company it is important to consider that it is possible to purchase an off-the-shelf company. This is a company that has already been incorporated and can be purchased, as opposed to creating a new company.

Key requirements

A private limited company requires a minimum of one director. There is no requirement that the company has a company secretary. A director must be aged 16 years or above.

Documents required by Companies House

Key definition: Companies House

The public body that is responsible for the creation and the dissolution of companies. It stores information, which companies have a legal obligation to supply, and the public are able to view this.

It is possible to establish (or incorporate) a company online at Companies House. Companies House requires that certain information be supplied. The company will require a registered office and this must be an address within the United Kingdom.

The INO1 form

There are a number of documents that must be supplied. The INO1 form must include the details of the directors and the company secretary and include information pertaining to their usual residential address, nationality, date of birth, occupation. The names and addresses of each shareholder who subscribes to the company must be included. Companies House will require information as to the number of shares issued, the class of shares, how much the share is worth and how much has been paid up for each share. The INO1 form also includes a certificate of compliance.

Memorandum of association

A memorandum of association must also be included. Where the company will have a share capital, then this document will confirm that each shareholder (or subscriber) intends to form the company and as a minimum take one share. The names of all the subscribers will be listed and they will confirm their intention.

Articles of association

The company will require articles of association. This is the company's constitution and will set out how it is intended that the company will be governed. This document is very important as it contains the rules for conducting company business, such as the percentage of shareholders required to take certain decisions. You do not need to draft your own articles of association as you can incorporate the model articles. For private companies that are limited by shares the previous model to use was called Table A and this has been replaced by the model articles in schedule 1 of the Companies (Model Articles) Regulations 2008.

Naming your company

Your company's name will clearly be important and when selecting a name you must be aware that you are not using the same name as an existing business, or that you do not infringe another business's intellectual property rights, i.e. if the name is a trademark, or that you are not liable for the tort of passing off. Companies House provides examples of names that would be too similar to existing names:

- where the names sound and look similar: Dynamic Technology Limited would be regarded as 'too like' Dinamix Teknology Limited;

- where there are differences in a couple of letters or characters: for example, International Logistic Support Limited and International Logistical Support Limited would be 'too like' but ICL plc & ICG plc would not.

It is important that the name of a company is not too similar to an existing name, as otherwise the company could be liable under the tort of passing off (see Chapter 5). The restrictions on what you can name a company are set out under ss.53–76 CA 2006.

You can carry out a search of existing company names on the Companies House website. If your proposed name contains sensitive words or expressions then you will require the Secretary of State's approach. Examples include where the company's name indicates a special function ('Institute'), a link with the government ('Cabinet Office'), or if it were to cause a criminal offence (such as using the word 'Solicitor' unless you are regulated by the Solicitors Regulatory Authority).

The registration fee

The fee for incorporating a company must also be included. At the time of writing the fee to incorporate a company online was £15.00 and for paper applications it was £20.00.

On-the-spot question

? Jennifer and Noor wish to establish a business selling tablet cases and accessories. They would like to know how they would establish a private company limited by shares and what documents would be required. Last week a supplier approached Jennifer and Noor and offered to sell them 4,000 tablet cases.

Would you advise Jennifer and Noor to enter into the contract either before, or after, the company was incorporated?

PUBLIC ACCESS

The information held by Companies House is available to the public (subject to some exceptions). This is important because where the company has limited liability potential suppliers, creditors and investors are able to ascertain the financial health of the company before doing business with it. Equally, competitors are able to use this information to their advantage. It is also possible to search against the names of the directors to see which other companies they have been a director for. The public can look at whether the company has met its filing requirements for its annual accounts and see how much profit has, or has not, been made.

On-the-spot question

? Donald Smith, a director of a new company, has approached Lucy and asked her to supply his company with £13,000 worth of stock. Donald stated that the company would pay Lucy 60 days after the contract was entered into. Lucy wants the business, but she is concerned about the company's financial health. She is sure that she has met Donald previously when he worked for another company and she is suspicious as to why he is working for this new company.

Advise Lucy on how she can use the register at Companies House to her advantage.

REPORTING REQUIREMENTS

The information held by Companies House will also include the annual return which must be submitted each year. If you do not submit the annual return then the company could be struck off. The annual return will contain current information pertaining to the subscribers, shareholding and directors. The company will also need to file annual accounts. Additionally, the company will need to submit information to Companies House including resolutions, changes to directors, charges (i.e. security for loans) and the company's constitution.

We can see that the reporting requirements are onerous. Focusing on a private company limited by shares, a small company with just two directors and three shareholders would be required to comply with these requirements.

TAXATION

A private company will pay corporation tax on its profits. The rate of corporation tax will depend on the profits made by a company. For example from 1 April 2014 the rate is 20 per cent where the profit is £300,000 or less, and 21 per cent where it is above £300,000. Once profits have been taxed the board of directors can decide to retain the money within the company as an asset or an investment. Alternatively, the board could decide to issue a dividend to shareholders. Each shareholder will pay income tax on the dividend that they receive. The advantage of paying corporation tax, as opposed to income tax as a sole trader, is that the amount of tax payable on any profits will be potentially lower under the corporation tax regime. However, in deciding which type of business is more beneficial in terms of taxation it is best to consult an accountant who can properly advise you. The following example demonstrates the differences between corporation tax and income tax:

- Brian is a sole trader and his business makes £120,000 profit in financial year 2014–15. Brian would pay income tax at 20 per cent for the first £34,370 which he makes (less his personal allowance which would be tax free). On any profit over £34,370 to £150,000 he would pay 40 per cent income tax. If Brian made over £150,000 then for any profit over that amount he would pay 50 per cent income tax.
- Brian sets up a company and is the sole shareholder. The company makes £120,000 profit in 2014–15. The company pays corporation tax at 20 per cent. Brian's salary as a director will be deducted before profits are calculated. Brian will pay income tax on his personal salary. If Brian wishes to issue a dividend in his capacity as a director then he will pay income tax on the dividend.

Directors will pay income tax (PAYE) on their salaries and shareholders will pay income tax on any dividends. Additionally, the company could be liable to pay capital gains tax (CGT) on the sale of any assets.

SEPARATE LEGAL PERSONALITY

Key definition: Separate legal personality

A business that has been incorporated at Companies House will have a separate legal personality to that of its owners. This means that the business will be regarded as a distinct legal person and can enter into contracts, purchase property, employ people, sue and be sued.

A company that has been incorporated at Companies House is regarded in law as having a separate legal personality. This is very important for a number of reasons. First, there will be a distinction between the company and the shareholders who own it. This means that if a private company limited by shares becomes insolvent, the maximum extent of a shareholder's personal liability will be their paid up or unpaid shareholding. The shareholder receives protection from unlimited personal liability.

This is an advantage over unincorporated businesses where there is no legal distinction between the business owner and the business. Consequentially, the business owner has unlimited personal liability.

The company is capable of owning property, employing staff, commencing legal action and of being sued. The company can also face criminal prosecution for offences such as corporate manslaughter (see the Corporate Manslaughter and Corporate Homicide Act 2007). Additionally, the company may own shares in another company or enter into a partnership.

As the company has a separate legal personality there is a risk that persons or businesses owed money by the company will receive nothing in the event that it becomes insolvent, notwithstanding the fact that its shareholders may be multi-millionaires. The most important decision regarding separate legal personality is *Salomon v Salomon & Co Ltd* [1897] AC 22.

KEY CASE ANALYSIS: *Salomon v Salomon & Co Ltd* [1897] AC 22

Background

Mr Salomon owned a business and decided to sell it to a private limited company that he had created in accordance with the Companies Act 1862. The company had seven shareholders, which included Mr Salomon who had 20,000 shares and his wife and children who had one share each. As part of the purchase price of the company Mr Salomon received a debenture, which was a floating charge over the company. This debenture would make Mr Salomon a priority creditor if the company became insolvent. Eventually the company became insolvent and the unsecured creditors were not paid as there was not enough money left once Mr Salomon's debenture was repaid. There was an attempt to have Mr Salomon indemnify the company. The Court of Appeal held that the creation of the company had been a sham to enable Mr Salomon to avoid personal liability and to have priority over other creditors via the creation of the debenture.

Principle established

The House of Lords held that as the company had met the requirement of the Companies Act 1862 it was validly created and therefore it had a separate legal personality and its liabilities were distinct from its shareholders. It was irrelevant that Mr Salomon had created the company to protect his business and that he was protected by the debenture. This decision is of utmost important as it protected the integrity of a company as being legally distinct from its owners.

In his judgment Lord Herschell considered the argument that the company had merely been created as an alias for Mr Salomon, and the other shareholders were just 'dummies' in order to meet the statutory requirements. His Lordship was unconvinced by these arguments:

> It is to be observed that both Courts treated the company as a legal entity distinct from Salomon and the then members who composed it, and therefore as a validly constituted corporation. This is, indeed, necessarily involved in the judgment which declared that the company was entitled to certain rights as against Salomon. Under these circumstances, I am at a loss to understand what is meant by saying that A. Salomon & Co., Limited, is but an 'alias' for A. Salomon. It is not another name for the same person; the company is ex hypothesi a distinct legal persona.
>
> . . .
>
> Here, it is true, Salomon owned all the shares except six, so that if the business were profitable he would be entitled, substantially, to the whole of the profits. The other shareholders, too, are said to have been 'dummies', the nominees of Salomon. But when once it is conceded that they were individual members of the company distinct from Salomon, and sufficiently so to bring into existence in conjunction with him a validly constituted corporation, I am unable to see how the facts to which I have just referred can affect the legal position of the company, or give it rights as against its members which it would not otherwise possess. (pp. 42–43)

Lord Halsbury LC had stated:

> Either the limited company was a legal entity or it was not. If it was, the business belonged to it and not to Mr Salomon. If it was not, there was no person and no thing to be an agent at all; and it is impossible to say at the same time that there is a company and there is not. (at p. 31)

DISTINCTION BETWEEN A DIRECTOR AND A SHAREHOLDER

A director is an officer of the company and together with the rest of the directors she will manage the company. In many small companies the shareholders will also be directors. The shareholders own the company. In larger companies the shareholders may not have much control over the company's affairs and, as we shall see below, the directors owe their duties to the company and not to the shareholders. The articles of association will state the types of shares in the company and their voting rights. Unlike a partnership under the Partnership Act 1890, a person can set up a company and subsequently resign as a director and still remain as a part owner of the business. This is because the owners of the company do not have to act as its managers.

The directors are appointed to manage the company and although the shareholders own the company, the directors will owe their duties to the company. The directors will have day-to-day control of the company and shareholders will be provided with the opportunity to vote on resolutions that can include removing a director and appointing a new director. The percentage of votes needed to pass certain types of resolutions will be determined in the articles of association. Ordinary resolutions require over 50 per cent support, whereas special resolutions require 75 per cent support. This means that a majority shareholder can exercise considerable power in a company and could prevent certain resolutions from being passed.

SHAREHOLDER LIABILITY

If you are a shareholder in a company limited by shares you will not be personally liable in the event that the company becomes insolvent. The only liability that a shareholder will have is their investment in the company which is represented by their shareholding. A shareholder will be liable for any shares that he has yet to pay up on. This is advantageous when contrasted with an unincorporated business.

On-the-spot question

Karl and Tom are the only shareholders in Restore Ur Car Ltd. They both own 50 shares at £2 each and have paid up the full amount. Karl is a multi-millionaire and Tom owns a castle in Kent. Restore Ur Car Ltd's assets are worth £23,000 and it has liabilities of £560,000.

Discuss Karl and Tom's liability as shareholders of Restore Ur Car Ltd.

PIERCING THE VEIL OF INCORPORATION

> ### Key definition: Veil of incorporation
>
> One of the key features of an incorporated company is that the law regards the company and its owners as being separate legal persons. If the company has been properly incorporated, then the courts will not treat the company's assets as belonging to its shareholders, or the company's actions as those of the shareholders, nor will they hold that the shareholders are personally liable for the company's liabilities. In certain circumstances the courts can pierce the veil of incorporation.

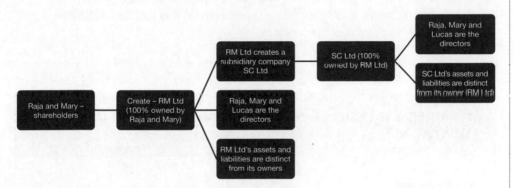

Figure 9.2 Parent and subsidiary companies

Scenario

Imagine that Raja and Mary decide to set up a business together and they have chosen to create a private company limited by shares. The company is called RM Ltd and the only shareholders are Raja and Mary. The directors of RM Ltd are Raja, Mary and Lucas. The board of directors decides to create a subsidiary company, SC Ltd. SC Ltd is created in order to pursue a new business venture, which in this economic climate might prove to be risky. SC Ltd will be wholly owned by RM Ltd which will be the only shareholder. Initially, the directors of SC Ltd will be Raja, Mary and Lucas.

On-the-spot question

After reading this section of the chapter please consider the following questions:

- If RM Ltd was to become insolvent what would Raja, Mary and Lucas' liabilities be?
- If SC Ltd was to become insolvent would RM Ltd, as the parent company, be liable for SC Ltd's debts?

Shareholders do not own the company's assets

It is important to note that a limited company that has been incorporated will have a separate legal personality. It will be legally distinct in terms of its liabilities and assets from the shareholders, who will own the company.

KEY CASE ANALYSIS: *Macaura v Northern Assurance Co Ltd* [1925] AC 619

Background

Mr Macaura owned a timber estate and decided to sell this to a company. He was the sole shareholder of the company. Unfortunately, he decided to insure the timber in his own name and not in the company's name. At a later date a fire destroyed the timber and he attempted to claim on the insurance policy.

Principle established

The House of Lords held that Mr Macaura could not recover under the insurance policy, as he had no insurable interest in the goods. The goods did not belong to him but rather to the company. Even as the sole shareholder he did not have any insurable interest. Lord Buckmaster stated that 'no shareholder has any right to any item of property owned by the company, for he has no legal or equitable interest therein' (at p. 626).

We have seen in *Salomon v Salomon* that the courts are not concerned with the shareholders and directors for the purposes of the company's liability. However, there may be circumstances when the courts will pierce the veil of incorporation and look at why the company had been created and hold the shareholder liable for avoiding a legal obligation or evading a restriction.

KEY CASE ANALYSIS: *Petrodel Resources Ltd v Prest* [2013] **UKSC 34; [2013] 2 AC 415**

Background

The decision involved a marital dispute. The wife alleged that her husband had transferred various properties in which he had a beneficial interest to a company in order to prevent the wife from obtaining a fair division of the marital assets.

Principle established

The Supreme Court held that piercing the corporate veil could be justified in certain circumstances in order to prevent a person from deliberately using a company to avoid an obligation or frustrating a legal restriction. But on the facts there was no evidence that this had been the husband's intention and therefore the court would not pierce the corporate veil. However, the court ordered that the properties must be transferred to the wife on the basis that on the available evidence it could be inferred that the husband was the beneficial owner. By ordering a transfer in these circumstances it did not pierce the corporate veil.

In the Court of Appeal's decision in *Prest v Petrodel Resources Ltd* [2012] EWCA Civ 1395, Rimer LJ had reiterated the distinction between the company and its shareholders:

> The judge noted . . . that 'a lay person' might think that a husband 'was entitled' to a house owned by a company that he owned. A lay person might so think but he would be wrong. If the same lay person carried on a business through a company of which he was the sole owner, and caused the company to incur liabilities that it could not meet, he would have no hesitation in asserting that the liabilities must be met exclusively by the company (by recourse exclusively to *its* assets) and (provided his shares were fully paid) had nothing to do with him personally. That is what limited liability is about. (at [102])

Fraudulent trading and the misapplication of assets

Exceptions that permit the court to pierce the corporate veil include where the company's assets are misapplied, or where there is wrongful or fraudulent trading (see ss.212–214 of the Insolvency Act 1986).

Setting up the company as a façade – the subsidiary company

Key definition: Subsidiary company

This is a company that is set up by a parent company to pursue a particular venture. The subsidiary company will protect the parent company from liability if the venture proves to be unsuccessful. The use of subsidiary companies is very common to shield the rest of the corporate group from financial loss and to minimise tax liability.

The Court of Appeal in *Adams v Cape Industries plc* [1990] Ch 433 considered in what circumstances the corporate veil could be pierced by the courts. The decision concerned whether a subsidiary company, that is a company created by another company, was a separate legal entity. If the court pierced the veil of incorporation then it would see that the shareholder of the subsidiary was the parent company, and would then proceed to hold the parent company liable. The court referred to the judgment of Lord Keith in *Woolfson v Strathclyde Regional Council* 1978 SLT 159, where it was held that the corporate veil could be pierced where it was apparent that the company was being used as a façade to conceal the true facts. The court noted that, in *Wallersteiner v Moir* [1974] 1 WLR 991, Lord Denning MR had argued that a subsidiary company was not 'a separate and independent entity'. However, the court observed that both Buckley LJ and Scarman LJ in Wallersteiner had disagreed with Denning MR on this point. The court observed '[w]e therefore think that the plaintiffs can derive little support from those dicta of Lord Denning MR'. The court asked whether the fact that the parent company was using the subsidiary company as a way to hide its involvement with the sale of asbestos and lawfully reducing its tax in the United States justified piercing the veil of incorporation. Its answer was no. Legally, there was nothing wrong with a corporate group setting up a company to shield the rest of the group from liability.

Criminal liability

In *Customs and Excise Commissioners v Hare* [1996] 2 All ER 391, the Court of Appeal held that the corporate veil could be lifted to charge individuals with criminal activity, as opposed to charging the company. Over a £100 million had not been paid in excise duty and the official receiver sought to recover assets. The court held that the assets were not in fact owned by the company, but rather they were owned by those who had engaged in criminal activity.

Avoiding obligations and breaching restrictions

We have seen in *Petrodel Resources Ltd* that the court will pierce the veil of incorporation where the company is being deliberately used to avoid a lawful obligation or to breach a restriction. In *Jones v Lipman* [1962] 1 WLR 832 the court lifted the veil of incorporation where the owner of land had agreed to sell land to the claimant. However, the owner changed his mind and established a company with the intention of frustrating the obligation to transfer the land. He subsequently sold the land to the company. The court ordered specific performance which compelled the defendant to transfer the land to the claimant. The court viewed the defendant and the company as not distinct. An example of a legal restriction being avoided was *Gilford Motor Co Ltd v Horne* [1933] Ch 935, where the defendant had worked for the claimant and was prevented by a restrictive covenant from competing against it. To avoid the restriction, the defendant set up a company. The company was held to be a sham and an injunction was awarded to prevent both the defendant and the company from competing with the claimant. Therefore, the court held there to be no distinction between the two.

Tortious liability

A director of a company may be liable personally where he makes a negligent misstatement to the claimant and there has been an assumption of personal responsibility by the director (see *Williams v Natural Life Health Foods Ltd* [1998] 1 WLR 830). A director may also be personally liable for a fraudulent misrepresentation as he will not be permitted to say that he committed the tort on behalf of the company (see *Standard Chartered Bank v Pakistan National Shipping Corp (No 2)* [2002] UKHL 43).

On-the-spot question

 Do you think that the decisions in *Jones v Lipman* and *Gilford Motor Co Ltd v Horne* were correctly decided?

WHO RUNS A COMPANY?

Key definition: Director

A director is responsible for the management of the company. A court may hold that a person is a director regardless of the title that he holds.

Key definition: Shareholder

A shareholder is a person who owns shares in a company. The shareholders may collectively own the company, but the company is legally distinct from them.

Key definition: Member

This refers to a shareholder. Members have certain rights under the Companies Act 2006.

The company is run by its directors. The number of directors required by a private limited company is one (s.155 CA 2006). Although, the company's articles of association may require that there is more than one director.

Definition of director

Section 250 CA 2006 defines a director as including 'any person occupying the position of director, by whatever name called'. If a director has been properly appointed to the company's board in accordance with the articles of association then she is known as a *de jure* director. If a director is appointed but there has been non-compliance with the articles of association then the director is known as a *de facto* director. In larger companies a director may be appointed not as an executive director, who is someone who is expected to devote their time to the managing of the company, but rather as a non-executive director who has been appointed to the board in order to advise at board meetings. A shadow director is someone who has not been appointed to the board but who seeks to control the management of the company from behind the scenes. Section 251 CA 2006 defines a shadow director as 'a person with whose directions or instructions the directors of the company are accustomed to act'. However, s.251(2) states that '(a) person is not to be regarded as a shadow director by reason only that the directors act on advice given by him in a professional capacity'. It is important to note that anyone who is regarded as being a director, regardless of their title or lack of official involvement with the company, can be held by the courts to owe to the company duties as a director (see below).

On-the-spot question

? Granny Mavis' two grandsons own 100 per cent of the shareholding in New Company Ltd. Every evening Granny Mavis listens to her grandsons discussing business matters and she frequently offers her advice on what they should do. The grandsons feel obliged to follow their grandmother's advice as they do not want to upset her.

Is Granny Mavis a director?

Board meeting

At the board meeting the directors will take decisions relating to the running of the company. The board meeting must be in quorum, this means that a minimum number of directors must be present. The articles of association will determine this number. The board can delegate certain decision-making powers to individual directors.

Managing director

The managing director will be responsible for the management of the company. A company does not need a managing director.

Chairman

The company does not need to have a full-time chairman: this is because a director can be appointed as the chair for a board meeting. A chairperson may be given a casting vote if there is an even split in the votes.

Shareholders

The shareholders at the annual general meeting (AGM) or extraordinary meetings will take important decisions. These decisions are made by ordinary or special resolutions and records of these must be sent to Companies House. The shareholders' involvement is needed to make changes such as to the articles of association (s.21 CA 2006), or to change the company's name.

Salary

Directors do not have to be paid a salary.

Are directors employees?

A director is not automatically an employee of the company. The employment status of a director would be determined with reference to any employment contract and other factors (see Chapter 7).

Do directors have the authority to bind the company?

A director is an agent of the company and can have the authority to bind the company in any contracts that she makes on the company's behalf. Whether a director does have the actual or apparent authority will depend on many factors including the articles of association, decisions taken by the board and whether the other party to the contract believed that the director had the authority to enter into a contract of that particular kind.

DIRECTORS' DUTIES

The CA 2006 codified the existing duties in common law and equitable principles that the director owed to the company (s.170(3)). A director is a fiduciary which means that he owes the company a number of very strict duties and these duties have now been codified by the CA 2006. Nonetheless, it is necessary to consider the case law here to interpret the statutory duties (s.170(4). These duties may also apply to a shadow director (s.170(5)). More than one duty can apply in any given situation (s.179). We will now consider each of these duties in turn.

s.171 Duty to act within powers

This provision states that the director must '(a) act in accordance with the company's constitution, and (b) only exercise powers for the purposes for which they are conferred'. This means that the director not only must not exceed his powers, but also he must not use these for an improper purpose. In determining whether there has been a breach, the court will consider why the powers were conferred on the director, to see if her apparently valid use of the powers breached s.171.

s.172 Duty to promote the success of the company

Under s.172(1), there is an obligation on the director to 'act in the way he considers, in good faith, would be most likely to promote the success of the company for the benefit of its members as a whole'. This links the success of the company and the shareholders who must ultimately benefit. The director must also have regard to a number of factors (a) to (f) which include the long-term consequences of the decision, the environmental impact and the need to act fairly between the shareholders.

s.173 Duty to exercise independent judgment

A director must not fetter her discretion and restrict her ability to take decisions in the future. This means that you cannot allow others to make decisions for you.

s.174 Duty to exercise reasonable care, skill and diligence

This section requires the director to exercise reasonable skills and diligence. Whether the director has fallen below the expected standard will be determined in accordance with what the 'reasonably diligent person with the general knowledge, skill and experience that may reasonably be expected of a person carrying out the functions carried out by the director in relation to the company' and the skills and experience the director himself possesses (s.174(2)). It is important to appreciate that if you are a director you must not lose interest in the company's day-to-day affairs. You are a director in order to act on behalf of the company and must fulfil your duties. If you wish to step back from the management of the company then you must resign as a director. However, if you are no longer a director then you will lose the ability to manage the company on a day-to-day basis. If you decide that you no longer wish to act as a director then if you still continue to take an interest in the management of the company you would still be regarded as a shadow director.

On-the-spot question

? Harvey is a director in a software development company and has worked in the industry for 15 years and is highly experienced. Mike has recently joined the company's board after spending three years working in the company's human resources department. Harvey and Mike are responsible for overseeing the development and sale of a software product. Unfortunately, things do not go well and the company is now suing both Harvey and Mike for failing to carry out their duties with reasonable care, skill and diligence.

Would Mike necessarily owe a lower duty of care than Harvey?

s.175 Duty to avoid conflicts of interest

The CA 2006 has reformed the existing law in relation to conflicts of interest as there will not be a conflict 'if the situation cannot reasonably be regarded as likely to give rise to a conflict of interest' (s.175(4)(a)). At common law, any possibility of conflict was enough to give rise to a breach of the duties owed and therefore it was no defence to argue that the reasonable person would not view the director's actions as giving rise to a conflict of interest (see *Boardman v Phipps* [1967] 2 AC 46). In *Boardman v Phipps*, Lord Upjohn dissented from the majority and had argued that there should be no breach where it would not be reasonably regarded as giving rise to a conflict of interest. The rationale for s.175 is to avoid a director entering into ventures that compete with the interests of the company. This duty does not just apply to working in competition, as it also applies to 'the exploitation of any property, information or opportunity (and it is immaterial whether the company could take advantage of the property, information or opportunity)' (s.175(2)). The inclusion of the fact that it would be immaterial whether the company could have taken the advantage replicates common law, where the courts have held that this is no defence (see *Regal (Hastings) Ltd v Gulliver* [1967] 2 AC 134). In *Industrial Development Consultants Ltd v Cooley* [1972] 1 WLR 443 the court held that a director who had resigned and subsequently took advantage of a contract that would never have been awarded to his former employer had breached his fiduciary duties and had to account for any profit that he had made.

KEY CASE ANALYSIS: *Bhullar v Bhullar* [2003] EWCA Civ 424

Background

In *Bhullar v Bhullar* [2003] a director of a grocery business had purchased a commercial property near to the company's premises which, although not a property that the company had intended to purchase, was nonetheless a good business opportunity.

Principle established

The court held that the director had breached his fiduciary duties as he had permitted a conflict of interest to arise between the company and his personal interests. It was immaterial that the company had not intended to purchase the company. The purchase was a good opportunity and was sufficiently proximate to the company's premises to have been a good investment.

The decision in *Bhullar* was followed in *Pennyfeathers Ltd v Pennyfeathers Property Co Ltd* [2013] EWHC 3530 (Ch). In this case the directors had used an opportunity owned by the company to purchase land. It was irrelevant that the company would not have pursued the opportunity itself. According to s.175(4)(b), a director will not have breached the duty that he owes under s.175 if his actions have been authorised by the board of directors.

On-the-spot question

? Do you think that it is right that a director should be liable under s.175 CA 2006 where she takes advantage of an opportunity that the company would never have chosen to exploit? Would it make a difference if the opportunity was in an area unrelated to the area that the company operated in?

When answering this question you should consider precisely who in a company decides whether to exploit an opportunity.

---

s.176 Duty not to accept benefits from third parties

This duty is not breached 'if the acceptance of the benefit cannot reasonably be regarded as likely to give rise to a conflict of interest' (s.176(4)). It is important to appreciate that benefits given in return for being awarded contracts could amount to a criminal offence under the Bribery Act 2010.

s.177 Duty to declare interest in proposed transaction or arrangement

If the director is aware that the company is entering into a transaction or an arrangement that he directly or indirectly has an interest in, then he must declare this interest to the board prior to the transaction taking place. Similarly to s.175(4)(a), an interest that cannot reasonably be regarded to amount to a conflict of interest does not need to be declared.

s.182 Declaration of interest in existing transaction or arrangement

This provision is similar to s.177 and a declaration of interest must be made as soon as the director becomes aware of this. Non-disclosure will amount to a criminal offence under s.183.

On-the-spot question

? Alfred is a director of Build It High Ltd (BIH Ltd). BIH Ltd is looking to purchase new premises. On 3 June, BIH Ltd's board of directors meets to vote on whether to purchase a warehouse owned by New Holdings Ltd (NH Ltd). Alfred is aware that he is a 35 per cent shareholder in NH Ltd. However, he decides that he does not need to tell the board as he will just stay quiet during the meeting and vote in accordance with what the majority of the directors have decided.

On 8 June, Ivor, BIH Ltd's sales director, meets with a supplier and during the meeting he is given tickets for an around the world cruise. Ivor accepts these and decides that no one needs to know about this. On 14 June, Ivor contracts to purchase stock worth £77,000 from the supplier.

Discuss any legal issues that have arisen here.

Protection from liability

The court has the power to relieve a director from liability (in whole, or part) where the director has breached his duties to the company, if the court believes 'that he acted honestly and reasonably, and that having regard to all the circumstances of the case (including those connected with his appointment) he ought fairly to be excused' (s.1157 CA 2006).

A note of caution

The director owes these duties to the company and if breached he could be sued by the company. Even if a director is currently the only shareholder and subsequently sells his shareholding, he could still in the future be potentially liable, if the new board of directors commences litigation against him on behalf of the company.

DIRECTORS' LIABILITY TO THIRD PARTIES

As discussed above, a director could be personally liable where he has made a fraudulent misrepresentation, commits a criminal offence or who makes a negligent misstatement and assumes personal responsibility to the third party. In addition, a director may be asked to give a personal guarantee before a bank will lend the company additional funds. If the director agrees to give a personal guarantee, then in the event that the company defaults on the loan the director will be personally liable.

COMPANY DIRECTORS DISQUALIFICATION ACT 1986

The Company Directors Disqualification Act 1986 (CDDA 1986) is there to regulate those persons who are unsuitable to act as a director. The court may order that a person is disqualified from being a director. This may be because the company has become insolvent and the court finds that he is unfit to be a director in the future (s.6 CDDA 1986). A director may be disqualified for reasons such as persistent breaches of his obligations under the CA 2006 (s.3 CDDA 1986) and having been convicted for committing a criminal offence (ss.2 and 5 CDDA 1986). Where there is a disqualification order and a person breaches this order and acts as a director, then he could be liable for a fine and face up to two years' imprisonment (s.13 CDDA 1986). Under s.6 a director of an insolvent company who has been held to be unfit by the courts may be disqualified from being a director for up to 15 years.

SHAREHOLDERS' RIGHTS

While the shareholders own the company this does not mean that a shareholder will manage the company's day-to-day affairs. A shareholder must become a director in order to do this. In reality a shareholder in many smaller companies may also be a director, as there is often just one director and one shareholder. The CA 2006 protects shareholders and permits them to have a say in important decisions.

Involvement in decision making

The CA 2006 will state that certain types of decisions require an ordinary or a special resolution. According to s.268(1) '[a]n ordinary resolution of the members (or of a class of members) of a company means a resolution that is passed by a simple majority'; whereas a special resolution 'means a resolution passed by a majority of not less than 75%' (s.283(1)). The company's articles of association could change the requirement for an ordinary resolution to a special resolution. The method of voting and the weighting of the shares owned would depend on how the vote will take place.

Shareholders are involved in decisions such as changing the company's articles, which requires a special resolution (s.21), or loaning money to a director, which requires an ordinary resolution (s.197(3)).

Each year there will be an annual general meeting that all shareholders must be invited to attend and to vote on decisions taken there. Additionally, it is possible to call a general meeting to take decisions. A general meeting can be called by the board of directors (s.302) and also by any shareholders who have more than 50 per cent of the voting rights in the company (s.305).

Approving substantial property transactions

We have seen above that a director must notify the board if there is a transaction in which he has a direct or indirect interest. The CA 2006 protects the shareholders by requiring that their permission is required before the company can enter into a substantial property transaction with a director or someone who is connected with the director (s.190). Section 191(2) states that an asset is substantial if it exceeds £100,000 or 10 per cent of the company's asset value so long as the asset is worth more than £5,000.

How a director can be dismissed

The shareholders can decide to dismiss a director or even the entire board. According to s.168 CA 2006 this can occur through an ordinary resolution.

Protection of minority shareholders

A shareholder who owns a minority of the shares may find that they feel that the company is not being run in a way that benefits them, or that the directors are breaching the duties that they owe to the company. The CA 2006 permits a shareholder to bring a derivative action where there has been a breach of a director's duties (s.260(3)). The shareholder is bringing the claim on behalf of the company, as the company is owed the duty that has been allegedly breached (s.260(1)). The shareholder needs to have the court's permission to bring a derivative claim and has the burden of demonstrating that there is a prima facie case for the court giving permission (s.261(2)). Section 264 states the factors that the court must take into account in deciding whether to permit a claim to be brought. These factors include whether the shareholder is acting in good faith and whether a person 'acting in accordance with section 172 (duty to promote the success of the company) would not seek to continue the claim'.

If a shareholder believes that the directors have been unfairly prejudicial to all of the members or a part of the members then she can petition to the court for an order to provide the claimant with relief (s.994–996). This relief could be to direct how the company regulates its affairs in the future, stop an act from occurring or order that an act does occur. The court could also allow civil proceedings to be brought in the company's name by the shareholder petitioning the court (see s.996).

On-the-spot question

Aisha own 15 per cent of the shares in TBC Ltd and is unhappy with the conduct of the directors. Aisha feels that she has been ignored and that she is concerned with the fact that the company is losing money. Ralph, one of the directors, is seldom in the office and spends his days playing golf, while Phoebe, the other director, is busy setting up her own business and never seems to respond to emails or telephone calls. Aisha is really good friends with David and Helen who each own 20 per cent of the shares in TBC Ltd.

Discuss the options that are available to Aisha.

Creation and the transfer of shares

A limited company must have shares that have a share capital that is fixed at a nominal value (s.542). Over time the company can create new shares to raise additional capital. In a private company that has only one class of shares, it is the directors, subject to the articles of association, who can take the decision to allot additional shares (s.550).

Section 544 states that the shares in a company are transferable in accordance with the articles of association. In a private limited company the shareholders may wish to transfer their shareholding to someone else. The CA 2006 states the requirements that must be met in order to do this. The articles of association may confer the directors with discretion to restrict the transfer of shares, such as allowing existing shareholders the right of first refusal.

Dividends

The dividend reflects the profits that the company has made. If the directors decide to award a dividend, then a shareholder has a right to receive this. There is no requirement that a dividend must be paid.

SUMMARY

- A limited liability partnership, a public limited company and a private limited company are types of incorporated business where the members enjoy limited liability.

- The Companies Act 2006 regulates both private and public companies. The duties owed by directors and the rights of shareholders are stated in the Act.
- The directors owe their duties to the company. The Companies Act 2006 has codified the directors' duties, although it is still necessary to consider the existing case law to understand how the courts will interpret these duties.
- A private limited company will be governed in accordance with its articles of association.

FURTHER READING

Dignam, A. and Lowry, J. *Company Law*, 7th edn (Oxford University Press, 2012) – you should refer to this book for a more detailed account of the material covered in this chapter.

Gray, A. 'The statutory derivative claim: an outmoded superfluousness?' [2012] 33(10) *Company Lawyer* 295 – an interesting article on the derivate claim under the Companies Act 2006.

Lim, E. 'Directors' fiduciary duties: a new analytical framework' (2013) 129 *Law Quarterly Review* 242 – you should refer to this article for a detailed consideration of directors' duties under the Companies Act 2006.

Sealy, L. 'The statutory statement of directors' duties: the devil in the detail' [2008] *Company Law Newsletter* 1 – this is a brief but authoritative overview of directors duties under the Companies Act 2006.

Sealy, L. and Worthington, S. *Sealy & Worthington's Cases and Materials in Company Law*, 10th edn (Oxford University Press, 2013) – this book is useful for those students who wish to explore company law in more detail.

Index